MONTAIGNE

LONGMANS' LIVING THOUGHTS LIBRARY

Volumes Already Published

ANDRÉ GIDE

CLITT LAMB

DEFOE ADDISON STEVENSON

PASCAL

VOLTAIRE

PLUTARCH

SaGrev

ROUSSEAU D'ALEMBERT CARLYLE RUSKIN

MONTAIGNE

THE LIVING THOUGHTS OF

MONTAIGNE

PRESENTED BY
ANDRÉ GIDE

THE LIVING THOUGHTS LIBRARY
EDITED BY ALFRED O. MENDEL

LONGMANS, GREEN AND CO.
NEW YORK · TORONTO

The Living Thoughts Library
is being published in Argentina (Spanish), Bulgaria, Canada, Czecho-
slovakia, Denmark, Finland, France, Great Britain, Hungary, Norway,
Poland, Rumania, Sweden, the United States of America, Yugoslavia

Translation of the Introductory Essay by Dorothy Bussy
The selections are from John Florio's translation

MONTAIGNE

First edition **March** 1939
Reprinted December 1943

9522

Life travels upward in spirals. He who takes pains to search the shadows of the past below us, then, can better judge the tiny arc up which he climbs, more surely guess the dim curves of the future above him.

MONTAIGNE

Montaigne is the author of a single book — the *Essays*. But in this one book, written without pre-conceived plan, without method, as events or his reading chanced to suggest, he claims to give us his whole self. He published four successive editions of it — the first in 1580, when he was forty-seven years old. This text he revised, he corrected, he perfected and, at his death in 1592, left yet another copy of his work loaded with emendations and ad-denda which were incorporated in later editions. Meanwhile Montaigne travelled through South Germany and Italy (1580–1581) and then filled the important post of Mayor of Bordeaux; he gives his readers the benefit of the observations he gath-ered in foreign lands and of the experiences of his public life at a period when the wars of religion were profoundly troubling his country.

From this time onwards, leaving public affairs in order to occupy himself only with his own thoughts, he shut himself up in his library and for the rest of his life never left the little château in Périgord where he was born. Here he wrote the additional chapters that constitute the third book of the *Es-says*; he revised the old ones, corrected, improved them and introduced six hundred additions. He occasionally encumbered his first text too with a load of quotations gathered in the course of his con-tinual reading; for Montaigne was persuaded that

1

everything had already been thought and said, and
was anxious to show that man is always and everywhere one and the same. The abundance of these
quotations which turn some of his chapters into a
compact pudding of Greek and Latin authors might
cast a doubt on Montaigne's originality. It must
indeed have been exceptionally great to triumph
over such a jumble of antiquities.

This show of erudition was not peculiar to Montaigne, for it was a time when men's heads had been
turned by Greek and Latin culture. Gibbon has
very justly remarked that the study of the classics,
which dates from much further back than the beginning of the Renaissance, retarded rather than
hastened the intellectual development of the peoples of the West. The reason for this is that writers
were then hunting for models rather than for inspiration and stimulus. Learning in the days of
Boccaccio and Rabelais weighed heavily on men's
minds and far from helping to liberate, stifled them.
The authority of the ancients, and of Aristotle in
particular, drove culture into a rut and during the
sixteenth century the University of Paris turned out
almost nothing but bookworms and pedants.

Montaigne does not go so far as to rebel against
this bookish culture, but he succeeded so well in
assimilating and making it his own that it was never
a hindrance to his mind, and in this he differs from
all other writers of his time. At most, he follows
the fashion by interlarding his works with quotations. But, "What availes it us," he asks, "to have
our bellies full of meat, if it be not digested ? If it
be not transchanged in us ? except it nourish, aug-
ment and strengthen us ?" (Bk. I, ch. 4.) And

again, and more prettily, he compares himself to the bees who "here and there suck this and cull that flower, but afterwards they produce the Honie which is peculiarly their own ; then is it no more Thyme or Marjoram."

The success of the *Essays* would be inexplicable but for the author's extraordinary personality. What did he bring the world then that was so new ? Self-knowledge — and all other knowledge seemed to him uncertain ; but the human being he discovers — and uncovers — is so genuine, so true, that in him every reader of the *Essays* recognizes himself.

In every historical period an attempt is made to cover over this real self with a conventional figure of humanity. Montaigne pushes aside this mask in order to get at what is essential ; if he succeeds it is thanks to assiduous effort and singular perspicacity ; it is by opposing convention, established beliefs, conformism, with a spirit of criticism that is constantly on the alert, easy and at the same time tense, playful, amused at everything, smiling, indulgent yet uncompromising, for its object is to know and not to moralize.

"Montaigne is the frankest and honestest of all writers," says Emerson, who places him among his constellation of six *Representative Men* with Plato, Swedenborg, Shakespeare, Goethe, and Napoleon. In his study on *Montaigne : or, the Skeptic*, he tells us that the *Essays* "is the only book which we certainly know to have been in the poet's library (the poet here being Shakespeare). "Leigh Hunt," he adds, "relates of Lord Byron, that Montaigne was the only great writer of past times whom he read with avowed satisfaction" ; and further on, "Gibbon reckons, in these bigoted times" (the sixteenth century) "but two men of liberality in France : Henry IV and Montaigne."

For Montaigne, the body is as important as the mind ; he does not separate the one from the other and is constantly careful never to give us his thoughts in the abstract. It is particularly incumbent on us therefore to see him before we listen to him. It is he himself who furnishes us with all the elements of a full-length portrait. Let us look at it.

He is rather short ; his face is full without being fat ; he wears a short beard according to the fashion of the period. All his senses are "sound, almost to perfection." Although he has used his robust health licentiously, it is still very hearty and only slightly affected by gravel at the age of forty-seven. His gait is assured, his gestures brusque, his voice loud and sonorous. He is fond of talking and always talks vehemently and excitedly. He eats of everything and anything so gluttonously that he sometimes bites his own fingers, for in those days forks were not in use. He rides a great deal and even in his old age he is not fatigued by long hours in the saddle. Sleep, he tells us, takes up a great portion of his life. And I would on no account omit a little detail which may make American readers smile : when he sits down, he likes to have his "legs as high as or higher than his seat." (Bk. III, ch. 13.)

The importance of an author lies not only in his personal value but also and greatly in the opportuneness of his message. There are some whose message is only of historical importance and finds no echo among us today. In past times, it may have stirred men's conscience, fed their enthusiasms, aroused revolutions ; we have no ears for it now. Great authors are not only those whose work answers to the needs of one country and one period, but those who provide us with a food which is able to satisfy the different hungers of various nationalities and successive generations. "A heedy reader," says Montaigne, "shall often discover in other men's compositions perfections farre different from the Author's meaning, and such as haply he never dreamed of, and illustrateth them with richer senses and more excellent constructions." (Bk. I, ch. 23.) Is he himself such an author and will he be able to answer such new questions as the "heedy reader" may wish to put to him ? I take leave to hope so.

In our time and in all countries whatsoever, constructive minds are in particular request ; the authors who are most admired are those who offer us a carefully composed system, a method for solving the agonizing political, social, and moral problems which are tormenting almost all peoples and every one of us individually. Montaigne, it is true, brings us no method (how could a method that might have been valid at his time be practicable in ours ?), no philosophical or social system. No mind could be less ordered than his. He lets it free to play and run wild as it pleases. And even his perpetual doubt which made Emerson consider him as the most perfect representative of skepticism (that is to say of antidogmatism, of the spirit of enquiry and investigation) may be compared, it has been said, to those purgative medicines which the patient ejects together with the stuff of which they rid him. So that some people have seen in his *"Que sçais-je ?"*

at once the highest mark of his wisdom and of his
teaching. Not that it satisfies me. It is not their
skepticism that pleases me in the *Essays,* nor is that
the lesson I draw from them. A "heedy reader"
will find in Montaigne more and better than doubts
and questions.

To Pilate's cruel question which re-echoes down
the ages, Montaigne seems to have assumed, though
in a quite human and profane manner, and in a very
different sense, Christ's divine answer : "*I am the
truth.*" That is to say he thinks he can know nothing *truly* but himself. This is what makes him talk
so much about himself ; for the knowledge of self
seems to him indeed as important as any other.
"The mask," he says, "must as well be taken from
things as from men." (Bk. I, ch. 19.) He paints
himself in order to unmask himself. And as the
mask belongs much more to the country and the
period than to the man himself, it is above all by
the mask that people differ, so that in the being that
is really unmasked, it is easy to recognize our own
likeness.

He even comes to think that the portrait he paints
of himself may be more generally interesting in proportion as it is more peculiar to himself ; and it is
by reason of this profound truth that we do in effect
take so great an interest in his portrait ; for "every
man beareth the whole stamp of human condition."
(Bk. III, ch. 2.) And more than this : Montaigne
is convinced that, "as Pindarus said, to be sincerely
true is the beginning of a great virtue." (Bk. II,
ch. 18.) These admirable words which Montaigne
borrowed from Plutarch, who himself took them
from Pindar, I adopt as my own ; I should like to

inscribe them in the forefront of the *Essays*, for there above all lies the important lesson I draw from them.

And yet Montaigne does not seem to have himself at first grasped the boldness and reach of this resolve of his to admit only the truth about himself and to paint himself as nature made him. This accounts for a certain early hesitation in his drawing, for his attempt to find shelter in the thick undergrowths of history, for his piling up of quotations and examples — authorizations, I was tempted to say — for his endless gropings. His interest in himself is at first vague and confused, with no very clear idea as to what is important, and with a suspicion that perhaps the things that are most negligible in appearance and the most commonly disdained may in reality be just those that are most worthy of attention. Everything in himself is an object of curiosity, amusement, and astonishment : "I have seen no such monster or more expresse wonder in this world than myself. With time and custom a man doth acquaint and enure himself to all strangeness ; but the more I frequent and know myself, the more my deformitie astonieth and the less I understand myself." (Bk. III, ch. 11.) And how delightful it is to hear him talking like this of his "deformitie," when what we like about him is precisely what enables us to recognize him as one of ourselves — just an ordinary man.

It is only when he gets to the third and last book of the *Essays* (which does not figure in the first edition) that Montaigne, in full possession, not of himself (he will never be that — no one can be) but of his subject, ceases to grope his way ; he knows

what he wants to say, what he must say, and he says
it admirably, with a grace, a playfulness, a felicity
and ingenuity of expression that are incomparable.
"Others," he says (speaking of moralists), "fashion
man, I relate him." And a few lines further on and
more subtly, "I describe not the essence but the
passage." (Bk. III, ch. 2.) (The Germans would
say the '*werden*'.) For Montaigne is constantly
preoccupied by the perpetual flux of all things, and
in these words he points to the non-stability of human personality which never *is*, but only conscious
of itself in the evanescent moment of *becoming*.
And as all other certainties break down around him,
this one at least grows greater and stronger, that
on this subject, at any rate — the subject of himself
— he is "the cunningest man alive" and that "never
man waded further into his subject, nor arrived
more exactly and fully to the end he proposed unto
himself" for which he has "neede of naught but
faithfulnesse" ; and he immediately adds "which is
therein as sincere and pure as may be found." (Bk.
III, ch. 2.)

I think the great pleasure we take in Montaigne's
Essays comes from the great pleasure he took in
writing them, a pleasure we feel, so to speak, in
every sentence. Of all the chapters that compose
the three books of the *Essays*, one alone is distinctly
tedious ; it is by far the longest and the only one he
wrote with application, care, and a concern for composition. This is the *Apology of Raymond Sebond*,
a Spanish philosopher who lived in the fifteenth century and professed medicine in France at the University of Toulouse, and whose *Theologia Naturalis*
Montaigne had laboriously translated at his father's

request. "It was a strange taske and new occupation for me : but by fortune being then at leisure and unable to gainsay the commandement of the best father that ever was, I came ere long (as well as I could) to an end of it." (Bk. II, ch. 12.) This chapter is the first that Montaigne wrote. It is one of the most celebrated and oftenest quoted, for Montaigne's mind, by nature so rambling and unorderly, here strives to develop a sort of doctrine and give apparent consistency to his inconsistent skepticism. But just because he is keeping his mind on the lead, it loses almost all its grace, the exquisite charm of its indolent progress ; he is directing it, we feel, towards an object, and we are never enchanted as we are later on when he allows it to venture tentatively down untraced paths and gather all the casually encountered flowers that grow by the wayside. No works, I should like here to remark, are more naturally perfect and beautiful than those which the author has most delighted in writing, those in which difficulty and effort are least apparent. In art, *seriousness* is of no avail ; the surest of guides is enjoyment. In all, or almost all, the other writings which go to make up the different chapters of the *Essays*, Montaigne's thought remains as it were in the fluid state, so uncertain, so changing, and even contradictory, that the most diverse interpretations of it were subsequently given. Some writers as, for instance, Pascal and Kant, attempt to see in him a Christian ; others, like Emerson, an exemplar of skepticism ; others a precursor of Voltaire. Sainte-Beuve went so far as to look upon the *Essays* as a sort of preparation, an antechamber to Spinoza's *Ethics*. But Sainte-Beuve seems to me nearest the truth when he says : "With an appearance of making himself out peculiar, of reducing himself to a bundle of odd manias, he has touched each one of us in his most secret part, and while portraying himself with careless, patient and incessantly repeated strokes, he has cunningly painted the majority of mankind, and all the more successfully as he has the more minutely dissected his single self — 'wavering and diverse' as he says. Each one of us finds a morsel of his own property in Montaigne. (*Port-Royal*, Bk. III, ch. 2.)

I consider it a mark of great strength in Montaigne that he succeeded in accepting his own inconsistencies and contradictions. At the beginning of the second book of the *Essays* the following sentence strikes the alarm : "Those which exercise themselves in controuling human actions, find no such difficulty in any one part as to piece them together and bring them to one same lustre ; for they commonly contradict one another so strangely, as it seemeth impossible they should be parcels of one warehouse." (Bk. II, ch. 1.) Not one of the great specialists of the human heart, be his name Shakespeare, Cervantes, or Racine, has failed to have at any rate fleeting glimpses of the inconsequence of human beings. But no doubt, it was necessary to establish for the time being a somewhat rudimentary psychology, on general and sharply defined lines, as a preliminary to the construction of a classical art. Lovers had to be nothing but lovers, misers wholly misers, and jealous men a hundred per cent jealous, while good care had to be taken that no one should have a share of all these qualities at once. Montaigne speaks of those "good authors" (and what he says is even truer of those who followed him than of those he was acquainted with) "who chuse an universal air and following that image, range and interpret all a man's actions; which, if they cannot wrest sufficiently, they remit them unto dissimulation." (Bk. II, ch. 1.) And he adds, "Augustus hath escaped their hands" much in the same tone as Saint-Evremond who, nearly a century later, says, "There are corners and twists in our soul which have escaped him [Plutarch]. . . He judged men too much in the rough and did not believe them to be so different from themselves as they are. . . What he thinks contradictory he attributes to external causes . . . which Montaigne understood far better." It seems to me that Montaigne, unlike Saint-Evremond, saw more than mere 'inconstancy'; I think that it is precisely under cover of this word that the real question lies hidden, and that it was not until much later that Dostoievsky, and then Proust, attacked it, so that some people say, "What is at issue here is the very conception of man on which we are now living," a conception which Freud and some others are now in process of breaking down. Perhaps the most surprising thing about Montaigne, the thing that touches us most directly, is those few, sudden lights he casts unexpectedly, and as it were involuntarily, upon the uncertain frontiers of human personality and upon the instability of the ego.

Montaigne's contemporaries no doubt skated over the few passages which shake us most today without having eyes to see them, or at any rate to judge of their importance. And no doubt Montaigne himself partly shared their indifference, just as he shared their curiosity for things which no longer interest us, and if he were to come back to earth today, he might very well say, "If I had known that that was what you would care about, there is a great deal more I might have told you!" Why in the world didn't you then? It was not your contemporaries it was important to please, but *us*. The points which were criticized or overlooked by his own epoch are often the very points by which a writer succeeds in reaching and communicating with us across the ages. To foresee in the midst of the day's preoccupations what will still deserve the interest of coming generations demands indeed peculiar penetration.

Love does not seem to have played much part in Montaigne's life; sensuality a greater one. He seems to have married without much enthusiasm. And if, in spite of this, he was a good husband, he nevertheless wrote towards the end of his life, "It is more easie to neglect and passe over all the sexe, than duely and wholly to maintain himself in his wife's companie" (Bk. II, ch. 33), which does not point exactly to his having done so. He had the lowest opinion of women, and beyond the pleasure he takes with them, confines them to the cares of the household. I have noted all the passages in the *Essays* in which he speaks of them; there is not one that is not insulting. And yet towards the end of his life he made an exception to this severity in favor of Mlle Marie de Gournay, his "daughter in alliance, and truly of me beloved with more than a fatherly love, and as one of the best parts of my being enfeofed in my home and solitariness." And he even adds, "There is nothing in the world I esteeme more than her." She was only twenty and Montaigne fifty-four when she was taken with an affection "more than superabounding" for the author of the *Essays.* It would be ungrateful not to mention this mutual attachment which was entirely spiritual in its nature, for it is to Mlle de Gournay's care and devotion that we owe the third and extremely important edition of the *Essays* (1595) which appeared three years after Montaigne's death, as well as the preservation of the manuscripts which served later for the establishment of the most authoritative text.

As to his own children, "they all die out at nurse," he tells us perfunctorily. (Bk. II, ch. 8.) An only daughter "escaped this misfortune," and these successive bereavements do not seem to have greatly affected him.

Montaigne, however, was by no means incapable of sympathy, and particularly towards small and humble folk : "I willingly give myself . . . unto the meaner sort . . . through some natural compassion, which in me is infinitely powerful." (Bk. III, ch. 13.)

But, for equilibrium's sake, his reason immediately demands a correction. "I have a very feeling and tender compassion of other men's afflictions, and should more easily weep for companie sake, if possible for any occasion whatsoever I could shed tears." (Bk. II, ch. 11.) La Rochefoucauld says at a later date, forestalling Nietzsche's famous "Let us be hard" : "I am little susceptible to pity and wish I were not so at all." But such declarations as these touch me particularly when they come from those who, like Montaigne and Nietzsche, are naturally tender-hearted.

Of Montaigne's sentimental life, friendship alone has left any trace in his work. Etienne de La Boëtie, his elder by three years, and author of a single short work entitled *On Voluntary Servitude*, inspired him with a feeling which seems to have occupied an important place in his heart and mind. This little book is not enough to make us consider La Boëtie "the greatest man of the age," as Montaigne did, but no doubt it helps us to understand the nature of the attachment which the future author of the *Essays* felt for a singularly generous and noble character.

Notwithstanding the beauty of this friendship, we may wonder whether it did not put some constraint upon Montaigne, and ask ourselves what the voluptuous author of the *Essays* would have been like if he had not met La Boëtie, and above all what the *Essays* would have been like if La Boëtie had not died so young (at the age of thirty-three) and if he had continued to exercise his influence over his friend. Sainte-Beuve, our great critic, quotes a very fine saying of the younger Pliny's : "I have lost the witness of my life. I fear I may henceforth live more carelessly." But this 'carelessly' is just what we like so much about Montaigne. Under La Boëtie's eyes, he draped himself a little in the antique fashion. In this, too, he was as sincere as ever, for he was greatly enamored of heroism ; but he did not like a man to be artificial, and liked it less and less ; more and more he came to fear that to grow in height must mean to increase in narrowness.

La Boëtie, in a piece of Latin verse addressed to Montaigne, says: "For you, there is more to combat, for you, our friend, whom we know to be equally inclined both to outstanding vices and virtues." Montaigne, when once La Boëtie had disappeared, withdrew more and more from the combat, as much from natural inclination as from philosophy. There is nothing Montaigne dislikes more than a personality — or rather an impersonality — obtained artificially, laboriously, contentiously, in accordance with morals, propriety, custom, and what he likens to prejudices. It is as though the true self which all this hampers, hides, or distorts, keeps in his eyes a sort of mystic value, and as if he were expecting from it some surprising kind of revelation. I understand, of course, how easy it is here to play upon words and to see in Montaigne's teaching nothing but a counsel to abandon oneself to nature, to follow one's instincts blindly, and even to grant precedence to the vilest, which always seem the sincerest, that is, the most natural, those which, by their very density and thickness are invariably to be found at the bottom of the recipient, even when the noblest passions have shaken it. But I believe this would be a very wrong interpretation of Montaigne who, though he concedes a large allowance, too large perhaps, to the instincts we have in common with animals, knows how to take off from them in order to rise, and never allows himself to be their slave or their victim.

It is natural that with such ideas, Montaigne should feel very little inclined to repentance and contrition. "I am grown aged by eight years since my first publications," he writes in 1588, "but I doubt whether I be amended one inch." (Bk. III, ch. 9.) And again: "The disorders and excesses

wherein I have found myself engaged, I have condemned according to their worth. But that is all."
(Bk. II, ch. 11.) Such declarations abound in the
last part of the *Essays*, and later on he adds again,
to some people's great indignation : "Were I to
live again, it should be as I have already lived. I
neither deplore what is past nor dread what is to
come." (Bk. III, ch. 2.) These declarations are
certainly as little Christian as possible. Every time
Montaigne speaks of Christianity it is with the
strangest (sometimes one might almost say with the
most malicious) impertinence. He often treats of
religion, never of Christ. Not once does he refer
to His words ; one might almost doubt whether he
had ever read the Gospels — or rather, one cannot
doubt that he never read them seriously. As for
the respect he shows Catholicism, there undoubtedly
enters into it a large amount of prudence. (We
must remember that the great massacre of Prot-
estants throughout the whole kingdom of France
on the eve of St. Bartholomew took place in 1572.)
The example of Erasmus (d. 1536) was a warning to
him, and it is easy to understand that he was far
from anxious to be obliged to write his *Retractions*.
I know that as a matter of fact Erasmus never did
write his, but he had to promise the Church that he
would. And even a promise of this kind is a nui-
sance. Far better to be wily.

In the editions of 1582 and 1595 a multitude of
conciliatory additions have been introduced into the
chapter entitled *Of Prayers and Orisons*. During
his travels in Italy in 1581, he had presented his book
to Pope Gregory XIII, who was the founder of
the Gregorian Calendar now in use. The Pope

complimented him but made a few reservations of which Montaigne took account in the passages he afterwards introduced into the *Essays*. In these, and in others as well, Montaigne insists to excess and with much repetition on his perfect orthodoxy and submission to the Church. The Church indeed showed herself at that time extremely accommodating ; she had come to terms with the cultural development of the Renaissance ; Erasmus, in spite of the accusation of atheism which caused his books to be condemned in Paris, was put up as a candidate for the Cardinalate ; the works of Macchiavelli, notwithstanding their profoundly irreligious character, had been printed in Rome by virtue of a 'brief' of Clement VII. This tolerance and relaxation on the part of the Church incited the great leaders of the Reformation to a corresponding increase of intransigence. Montaigne could come to an understanding with Catholicism but not with Protestantism. He accepted religion provided it was satisfied with a semblance. What he wrote about princes applied in his mind to ecclesiastical authorities as well : "All inclination and submission is due to them, except the mind's. My reason is not framed to bend or stoop ; my knees are." (Bk. III, ch. 8.)

In order still further to protect his book, he felt impelled to insert further passages of a very reassuring nature, in which he is hardly recognizable, into those very parts of the *Essays* which are most likely to arouse alarm in the hearts of sincere Christians : "This only end of another life, blessedly immortal, doth rightly merit we should abandon the pleasures and commodities of this our life." (Bk. I, ch. 38.) This passage (which for that matter

was left in manuscript and only published after
his death) and other similar ones seem to have
been stuck into his book like so many lightning-
conductors, or better still, like labels of lemonade
or ginger-ale fixed upon bottles of whiskey when a
régime has gone dry. And in fact a few lines after
the lightning-conductor come the words: "We must
tooth and naile retain the use of this life's pleasures,
which our years snatch from us one after another."

This passage of the first edition, which the added
lines attempt in vain to disguise, shows the true
Montaigne, that "sworne enemy to all falsifications"
(Bk. I, ch. 39) ; and I should be indignant at this
cautious recantation, if I did not think that it had
perhaps been necessary in order to get his wares
safely through to us. Sainte-Beuve says of him
very justly : "He may have appeared a very good
Catholic except for not having been a Christian."
So that one might say of Montaigne what he himself
said of the Emperor Julian : "In matter of religion
he was vicious everywhere. He was surnamed the
Apostate because he had forsaken ours ; notwithstanding, this opinion seems to me more likely, that
he never took it to heart, but that for the obedience
which he bare to the law he dissembled." (Bk. III,
ch. 19.) And later, quoting Marcellinus, again
about Julian : "He hatched Paganism in his heart
but forasmuch as he saw all those of his army to be
Christians, he durst not discover himself." (ibid.)
What he likes about Catholicism, what he admires
and praises, is its order and ancientness. "In this
controversie by which France is at this instant mo-
lested with civil warres, the best and safest side is
no doubt that which maintains both the ancient

religion and policy of the country," he says. (Bk. II, ch. 19.) For "all violent changes and great alterations, disorder, distemper and shake a state very much." And "the oldest and best known evil is ever more tolerable than a fresh and unexperienced mischief." (Bk. III, ch. 9.) There is no need to look for any other explanation of his ignorance of the Gospels and his hatred of Protestant reformers. He wishes to keep the Church's religion — France's religion — as it is, not because he thinks it the only good one but because he thinks it would be bad to change it.

In the same way we feel throughout Montaigne's life and writings a constant love of order and moderation, care for the public good, a refusal to let his own personal interest prevail over the interest of all. But he believes that the honesty of his own judgment and the preservation of that honesty are more valuable than any other considerations and should be set above them. "I would rather let all affairs go to wracke than to force my faith and conscience for their availe." (Bk. II, ch. 17.) And I prefer to believe in the sincerity of this statement rather than ask myself whether he is not bragging a little ; for it is as important nowadays that such words should be listened to as it was important in Montaigne's troubled times that there should be men to keep the integrity of their conscience and maintain their independence and autonomy above the herd instincts of submission and cowardly acceptance. "All universal judgements are weak, demisse [loose] and dangerous." (Bk. III, ch. 8) ; or again : "There is no course of life so weake and sottish as that which is managed by Order, Method and Discipline."

(Bk. III, ch. 13.)   Passages of this kind abound in the *Essays*, and as they seem to me of the highest importance, particularly nowadays, I will quote one more : "The Commonwealth requireth some to betray, some to lie," (and, alas ! he was obliged to add later) "and some to massacre : leave we that commission to people more obedient and more pliable." (Bk. III, ch. 1.)

When he resigned his post of magistrate and later on, too, when he left the mayoralty of Bordeaux to occupy himself henceforth exclusively with himself, he judged very rightly that the elaboration of his *Essays* would be the greatest service he could render to the State, and — let me add — to all mankind. For it must be observed that the idea of mankind for Montaigne predominates greatly over that of country. After a wonderful panegyric of France, or at any rate of Paris, "the glory of France and one of the noblest and chief ornaments of the world" which "I love so tenderly that even her spots, her blemishes and her warts are dear to me" (Bk. III, ch. 9), he takes care to say that his love of the human race is greater still. . . "I esteeme all men as my countrymen ; and as kindly embrace a Polonian as a Frenchman, postponing this natural bond to universal and common" (ibid.). "Friendships," he adds, "merely acquired by ourselves do ordinarily exceed those to which we are joyned either by communication of climate or affinity of blood. Nature hath placed us in the world free and unbound ; we emprison ourselves into certain streights, as the Kings of Persia, who bound themselves never to drinke of other water than of their river Choaspez, foolishly renouncing all lawful right of use in all other waters,

and for their regard dried up all the rest of the
world." (ibid.)

"Each of us inevitable ;
 Each of us limitless ; each of us with his or her right
    upon the earth"

says Walt Whitman.   (Ah ! how Montaigne would
have delighted — Montaigne who was so unblushing
on the subject of his person, so anxious not to oppose
the soul to the flesh and to proclaim the latter's legiti-
mate and healthy pleasures — how he would have delighted to hear Whitman sing, indecently and gloriously, the beauties and robust joys of his body !)
    One never comes to an end with Montaigne.   As
he speaks of everything without order or method,
any man can glean what he likes from the *Essays,*
which will often be what some other would leave
aside.   There is no author it is easier to give a twist
to without incurring the blame of betraying him,
for he himself sets the example and constantly con-
tradicts and betrays himself.   "Verilie (and I feare
not to avouch it), I could easily for a neede bring a
candle to Saint Michael and another to his Dragon."
(Bk. III, ch. 1.)   This, it must be admitted, is more
likely to please the Dragon than Saint Michael.
Montaigne, indeed, is not beloved by partisans,
whom he certainly did not love, which explains why
he was not held in much favor after his death, in
France, at any rate, which was torn in two by the
bitterest factions.   Between 1595 (he died in 1592)
and 1635, there were only three or four re-editions
of the *Essays.*   It was abroad, in Italy, in Spain, and
particularly in England, that Montaigne soon be-

came popular during this period of French disfavor or semi-favor. In Bacon's *Essays* and Shakespeare's plays there are unmistakable traces of Montaigne's influence.

It is well known that there exists in the British Museum a copy of Florio's translation of Montaigne which bears one of the rare signatures of the author of *Hamlet*. It is in this play in particular that English critics have found traces of Montaigne's philosophy. And in *The Tempest* he makes Gonzalo say :

"Had I plantation of this isle . . .
  And were the king on't, what would I do ? . . .
  I' the common wealth I would by contraries
  Execute all things ; for no kind of traffic
  Would I admit ; no name of magistrate ;
  Letters should not be known ; riches, poverty,
  And use of service, none ; contract, succession,
  Bourn, bound of land, tilth, vineyard, none ;

  .   .   .

  No occupation ; all men idle, all ;
  And women too, but innocent and pure ;
  No sovereignty. . .
  All things in common nature should produce
  Without sweat or endeavour ; treason, felony,
  Sword, pike, knife, gun, or need of any engine,
  Would I not have ; but nature should bring forth,
  Of its own kind, all foison, all abundance,
  To feed my innocent people."

Act II, Sc. I.

This passage is practically translated, or at any rate greatly inspired by a chapter of the *Essays* of which an extract will be found in the following pages. Everything that Montaigne says here on

Cannibals — the title of this chapter — will no doubt particularly interest Americans, for his subject is the New World which had been recently discovered, and towards which Europe was turning ecstatic glances. It hardly matters that countless illusions went to make up the prestige of these distant lands. Montaigne delights in describing their inhabitants and the purity of their manners and customs, just as Diderot, two centuries later, painted the manners of the Tahitians in order to shame those of the Old World. Both the one and the other understand what instruction and guidance the whole of humanity might gather from the sole example of a happy man.

In his drift away from Christianity, it is to Goethe that Montaigne draws near by anticipation. "As for me who love life and cultivate it, such as it hath pleased God to grant it us. . . Nature is a gentle guide, yet not more gentle than prudent and just." (Bk. III, ch. 13.) Goethe would no doubt gladly have endorsed these sentences which are almost the last of the *Essays*. This is the final flowering of Montaigne's wisdom. Not a word of it is useless. How very careful he is to add the idea of prudence, justice, and culture to his declaration of the love of life !

What Montaigne teaches us especially is what was called at a much later date, *liberalism*, and I think that it is the wisest lesson that can be drawn from him at the present time when political or religious convictions are so miserably dividing all men and opposing them to each other. "In the present intestine trouble of our State my interest hath not made me forget neither the commendable qualities of our adversaries, nor the reproachful of those I have followed." (Bk. III, ch. 10.) He adds a little later : "A good Oratour loseth not his grace by pleading against me." (ibid.) And further on these admirable lines : "They will . . . our perswasion and judgement serve not the truth but the project of our desires. I should rather erre in the other extremitie, so much I fear my desire might corrupt me. Considering I somewhat tenderly distrust myself in things I most desire." (ibid.) These qualities of mind and soul are never more wanted and would never be of greater service than at the times when they are most generally disregarded.

This rare and extraordinary propensity, of which he often speaks, towards listening to, and even espousing, other people's opinions, to the point of letting them prevail over his own, prevented him from venturing very far along the road that was afterwards to be Nietzsche's. He is held back by a natural prudence from which, as from a safeguard, he is very loth to depart. He shrinks from desert places and regions where the air is too rarefied. But a restless curiosity spurs him on, and in the realm of ideas he habitually behaves as he did when travelling. The secretary who accompanied him on his tour kept a journal. "I never saw him less tired," he writes, "nor heard him complain less of his pain," (he suffered at that time from gravel, which did not prevent him from remaining for hours in the saddle) "with a mind, both on the road and in our halting places, so eager for any encounters, so on the lookout for opportunities to speak to strangers, that I think it distracted him from his ills." He declared he had "no project but to perambulate through unknown places," and further, "He took such great pleasure in travelling that he hated the neighbourhood of the place where he was obliged to rest." Moreover, he "was accustomed to say that after having passed a restless night, when in the morning it came to his mind he had a town or new country to visit, he would rise with eagerness and alacrity." He himself writes in his *Essays* : "Well I wot that being taken according to the bare letter, the pleasure of travelling brings a testimony of unquietness and irresolution, which, to say truth, are our mistress and predominant qualities. Yes, I confesse it : I see nothing but in a dream or by wishing, wherein I may lay hold. Only variety and possession of diversitie doth satisfy me, if at least anything satisfy me." (Bk. III, ch. 9.)

Montaigne was very nearly fifty years old when he undertook the first and only long journey of his life through South Germany and Italy. This journey lasted seventeen months and in all probability would have lasted still longer, considering the extreme pleasure he took in it, if his unexpected election to the mayoralty of Bordeaux had not suddenly recalled him to France. From that moment he directed towards ideas the high-spirited curiosity that had sent him hurrying along the roads.

It is very instructive to follow through the successive editions of the *Essays* the modifications of his attitude towards death. He entitles one of the first chapters of his book, "That to Philosophise is to learn how to Die" in which we read : "There is nothing wherewith I have ever more entertained myself than with the imaginations of death, yea, in the most licentious times of my age." (Bk. I, ch.

19.) His idea was that, by familiarizing himself with these imaginations, he would diminish their horror. But in the last edition of his *Essays* he reached the point of saying : "I am now by meanes of the mercy of God . . . without regret or grieving at any worldly matter prepared to dislodge whensoever he shall please to call me. I am everywhere free ; my farewell is soon taken of all my friends, except of myself. No man did ever prepare to quit the world more simply and fully, or more universally left all thoughts of it than I am assured I shall do . . . nor can death put me in mind of any new thing." (Bk. I, ch. 19.) He almost gets to love this death as he loves all that is natural.

We are told that Montaigne made a very Christian end. All we can say is that he was by no means on the road to it. It is true that his wife and daughter were present at his last moments and no doubt they induced him, out of sympathy, as often happens, to die, not that "death united in itself, quiet and solitarie, wholly mine, convenient to my retired and private life," with which he would have been "content," but more devoutly than he would have done of himself. Is it a presentiment of this that made him write, "If I were to chuse, I thinke it should rather be on horseback than in a bed, farre from my home, farre from my friends"? (Bk. III, ch. 9.)

If I am accused of having sharpened Montaigne's ideas to excess, my answer is that numbers of his commentators have busied themselves with blunting them. I have merely removed their wrappings and disengaged them from the wadding that sometimes chokes the *Essays* and prevents their shafts from reaching us. The great preoccupation of pedagogues, when they are faced with authors of some boldness who yet are classics, is to render them inoffensive ; and I often wonder that the work of years should so naturally contribute to this. After a little it seems as though the edge of new thoughts gets worn away, and on the other hand, from growing in some sort accustomed to them, we are able to handle them without fear of injury.

Montaigne, during his travels in Italy, is often surprised to see the loftiest monuments of ancient Rome half buried in a mass of fallen litter. Their summits have been the first to crumble and it is their own fragments that strew the earth around them and gradually raise its level. If, in our day, they do not seem to tower so high above us, it is also because we do not stand so far below them.

André Gide has selected and arranged the
essence of Montaigne's thought from

THE *ESSAYS*

TRANSLATED BY JOHN FLORIO

1603

"Tout abrégé d'un bon livre est un sot abrégé."
— Montaigne, *Essays*, Bk. III, ch. 8

THE AUTHOR TO THE READER

Reader, loe here a well-meaning Booke. It doth at the first entrance forewarne thee, that in contriving the same I have proposed unto my selfe no other than a familiar and private end : I have no respect or consideration at all, either to thy service, or to my glory : my forces are not capable of any such desseigne. I have vowed the same to the particular commodity of my kinsfolk and friends : to the end, that losing me (which they are likely to do ere long), they may therein find some lineaments of my conditions and humours, and by that meanes reserve more whole, and more lively foster the knowledge and acquaintance they have had of me. Had my intention beene to forestal and purchase the world's opinion and favour, I would surely have adorned myselfe more quaintly, or kept a more grave and solemne march. I desire therein to be delineated in mine own genuine, simple and ordinarie fashion, without contention, art or study ; for it is myselfe I pourtray. My imperfections shall therein be read to the life, and my naturall forme discerned, so farreforth as publike reverence hath permitted me. For if my fortune had beene to have lived among those nations which yet are said to live under the sweet liberty of Nature's first and uncorrupted lawes, I assure thee, I would most willingly have pourtrayed myselfe fully and naked. Thus, gentle Reader, myselfe am the groundworke of my booke : it is then no reason thou shouldest employ thy time about so frivolous and vaine a subject.

Therefore farewell.

From MONTAIGNE,

The First of March, 1580.

THE *ESSAYS* OF MONTAIGNE

How Montaigne came to write his Essays

It is not long since I retired myselfe unto mine owne house, with full purpose, as much as lay in me, not to trouble myselfe with any businesse, but solitarily and quietly to weare out the remainder of my well-nigh-spent life ; where me thought I could doe my spirit no greater favour, than to give it the full scope of idlenesse, and entertaine it as he best pleased, and withall, to settle itselfe as it best liked : which I hoped it might now, being by time become more setled and ripe, accomplish very easily : but I finde, that contrariwise playing the skittish and loose-broken jade, it takes a hundred times more cariere and libertie unto itselfe, than it did for others, and begets in me so many extravagant Chimeraes, and fantasticall monsters, so orderlesse, and without any reason, one hudling upon another, that at leasure to view the foolishnesse and monstrous strangenesse of them, I have begun to keepe a register of them, hoping, if I live, one day to make it ashamed, and blush at itselfe.

Bk. I, ch. 8, *Of Idlenesse*

Reflections on Death

The end of our cariere is death, it is the necessarie object of our aime : if it affright us, how is it possible we should step one foot further without an ague ? The remedie of the vulgar sort is, not to think on it. But from what brutall stupiditie may so grosse a blindnesse come upon him? . . .

But it is folly to thinke that way to come unto it. They come, they goe, they trot, they daunce: but no speech of death. All that is good sport. But if she be once come, and on a sudden and openly surprise, either them, their wives, their children, or their friends, what torments, what out-cries, what rage, and what despaire doth then overwhelme them? saw you ever anything so drooping, so changed, and so distracted? A man must looke to it, and in better times fore-see it. And might that brutish carelessenesse lodge in the minde of a man of understanding (which I find altogether impossible) she sels us her ware at an overdeere rate: were she an enemie by mans wit to be avoided, I would advise men to borrow the weapons of cowardlinesse: but since it may not be, and that be you either a coward or a runaway, an honest or valiant man, she overtakes you . . . and that no temper of cuirace may shield or defend you, . . . let us learne to stand, and combat her with a resolute minde. . . There belongs more to it: Nature her selfe lends her hand, and gives us courage. If it be a short and violent death, wee have no leisure to feare it; if otherwise, I perceive that according as I engage my selfe in sicknesse, I doe naturally fall into some disdaine and contempt of life. I finde that I have more adoe to digest this resolution, that I shall die when I am in health, than I have when I am troubled with a fever: forsomuch as I have no more such fast hold on the commodities of life, whereof I begin to lose the use and pleasure, and view death in the face with a lesse undanted looke, which makes

me hope, that the further I goe from that, and the
nearer I approch to this, so much more easily doe I
enter in composition for their exchange. Even as
I have tried in many other occurrences, which Cæsar
affirmed, that often some things seeme greater, being
farre from us, than if they bee neere at hand : I have
found that being in perfect health, I have much
more beene frighted with sicknesse, than when I
have felt it. The jollitie wherein I live, the pleasure
and the strength make the other seeme so dispropor-
tionable from that, that by imagination I amplifie
these commodities by one moitie, and apprehended
them much more heavie and burthensome, than I
feele them when I have them upon my shoulders.
The same I hope will happen to me of death. . .

A man should designe nothing so long afore hand,
or at least with such an intent, as to passionate himselfe to see the end of it ; we are all borne to be doing.

I would have a man to be doing, and to prolong
his lives offices as much as lieth in him, and let death
seize upon me whilest I am setting my cabiges, carelesse of her dart, but more of my unperfect garden.

Bk. I, ch. 19, *That to Philosophise is to learn how to Die*

Custom

The laws of conscience, which we say to proceed
from nature, rise and proceed of custome : every
man holding in special regard and inward veneration
the opinions approved, and customes received about
him, cannot without remorse leave them, nor without applause applie himselfe unto them. . . But
the chiefest effect of her power is to seize upon us,

and so to entangle us, that it shall hardly lie in us to
free ourselves from her hold-fast, and come into
our wits againe, to discourse and reason of her ordinances ; verily, because we sucke them with the
milke of our birth, and forasmuch as the worlds visage presents itselfe in that estate unto our first view,
it seemeth we are borne with a condition to follow
that course.   And the common imaginations we
finde in credit about us, and by our fathers seed in-
fused in our soule, seeme to be the generall and naturall.   Whereupon it followeth, that whatsoever is
beyond the compasse of custome, wee deeme likewise to bee beyond the compasse of reason, God
knowes how for the most part, unreasonably. . .
But men receive the admonitions of truth and her
precepts, as directed to the vulgar, and never to
themselves ; and in lieu of applying them to their
maners, most men most foolishly and unprofitably
apply them to their memorie.   But let us returne to
customes soveraignty : such as are brought up to
libertie, and to command themselves, esteeme all
other forme of policie as monstrous and against nature.   Those that are enured to Monarchie doe the
like.   And what facilitie soever fortune affoordeth
them to change, even when with great difficultie
they have shaken off the importunitie of a tutor,
they run to plant a new one with semblable difficulties, because they cannot resolve themselves to hate
tutorship.   It is by the meditation of custome that
every man is contented with the place where nature
hath setled him ; and the savage people of Scotland
have nought to do with Touraine ; nor the Scithians
with Thessalie. . . Custome doth so bleare us that
we cannot distinguish the true visage of things. . .

Hee that will free himselfe from this violent prejudice of custome, shall find divers things received with an undoubted resolution, that have no other anker but the hoarie head and frowning wimples of custom, which ever attends them : which maske being pulled off, and referring all matters to truth and reason, he shall perceive his judgment, as it were overturned, and yet placed in a much surer state. . . These considerations do neverthelesse never distract a man of understanding from following the common guise. Rather, on the contrary, mee seemeth that all severall, strange, and particular fashions proceed rather of follie or ambitious affectation than of true reason : and that a wise man ought inwardly to retire his minde from the common presse, and hold the same liberty and power to judge freely of all things, but for outward matters he ought absolutely to follow the fashions and forme customarily received. Publike societie hath nought to do with our thoughts ; but for other things, as our actions, our travel, our fortune, and our life, that must be accommodated and left to its service and common opinions ; as that good and great Socrates, who refused to save his life by disobeying the magistrate, yea a magistrate most wicked and unjust. For that is the rule of rules, and generall law of lawes, for every man to observe those of the place wherein he liveth.

Bk. I, ch. 22, *Of Custome, and how a received law should not easily be changed*

Of Education

I never knew father, how crooked and deformed soever his sonne were, that would either altogether cast him off, or not acknowledge him for his owne :

and yet (unlesse he be meerely besotted or blinded in his affection) it may not be said, but he plainly perceiveth his defects, and hath a feeling of his imperfections. But so it is, he is his owne. So it is in my selfe. I see better than any man else, that what I have set downe is nought but the fond imaginations of him who in his youth hath tasted nothing but the paring, and seen but the superficies of true learning : whereof he hath retained but a generall and shapelesse forme : a smacke of every thing in generall, but nothing to the purpose in particular : After the French manner. To be short, I know there is an art of Phisicke ; a course of lawes ; foure parts of the Mathematikes ; and I am not altogether ignorant what they tend unto. And perhaps I also know the scope and drift of Sciences in generall to be for the service of our life. But to wade further, or that ever I tired my selfe with plodding upon Aristotle (the Monarch of our moderne doctrine) or obstinately continued in search of any one science : I confesse I never did it. Nor is there any one art whereof I am able so much as to draw the first lineaments. And there is no scholler (be he of the lowest forme) that may not repute himselfe wiser than I, who am not able to oppose him in his first lesson : and if I be forced to it, I am constrained verie impertinently to draw in matter from some generall discourse, whereby I examine, and give a guesse at his naturall judgement : a lesson as much unknowne to them as theirs is to me. . .

. . . My conceits, and my judgement march but uncertaine, and as it were groping, staggering, and stumbling at every rush : And when I have gone as far as I can, I have no whit pleased my selfe : for

the further I saile the more land I descrie, and that
so dimmed with fogges, and overcast with clouds,
that my sight is so weakned, I cannot distinguish the
same.

Choice of a Tutor

To a gentleman borne of noble parentage, and
heire of a house that aymeth at true learning, and in
it would be disciplined, not so much for game or
commoditie to himselfe (because so abject an end is
far unworthie the grace and favour of the Muses,
and besides, hath a regard or dependencie of others)
nor for externall shew and ornament, but to adorne
and enrich his inward minde, desiring rather to
shape and institute an able and sufficient man, than
a bare learned man ; my desire is therefore, that the
parents or overseers of such a gentleman be very
circumspect, and careful in chusing his director,
whom I would rather commend for having a well
composed and temperate braine, than a full stuft
head, yet both will doe well.   And I would rather
prefer wisdome, judgement, civill customes, and
modest behaviour, than bare and meere literall learning ; and that in his charge he hold a new course.
Some never cease brawling in their schollers eares
(as if they were still pouring in a tonell) to follow
their booke, yet is their charge nothing else but to
repeat what hath beene told them before.   I would
have a tutor to correct this part, and that at first entrance, according to the capacitie of the wit he hath
in hand, he should begin to make shew of it, making
him to have a smacke of all things, and how to
choose and distinguish them, without helpe of oth-

ers, sometimes opening him the way, other times leaving him to open it by himselfe. I would not have him to invent and speake alone, but suffer his disciple to speak when his turne cometh . . .

. . . And truly in barring him of libertie to doe any thing of himselfe, we make him thereby more servile and more coward. . . In this schoole of commerce, and societie among men, I have often noted this vice, that in lieu of taking acquaintance of others, we only endevour to make our selves knowne to them : and we are more ready to utter such merchandize as we have, than to ingrosse and purchase new commodities. Silence and modestie are qualities very convenient to civil conversation. . . That he be taught to be curious in making choice of his reasons, loving pertinency, and by consequence brevitie. That above all, he be instructed to yeeld, yea to quit his weapons unto truth, as soone as he shall discerne the same, whether it proceed from his adversarie, or upon better advice from himselfe ; for . . . I would faine have Paluel or Pompey, these two excellent dauncers of our time, with all their nimblenesse, teach any man to doe their loftie tricks and high capers, only with seeing them done, and without stirring out of his place, as some Pedanticall fellowes would instruct our minds without moving or putting it in practice. And glad would I be to find one that would teach us how to manage a horse, to tosse a pike, to shoot-off a peece, to play upon the lute, or to warble with the voice, without any exercise, as these kind of men would teach us to judge, and how to speake well, without any exercise of speaking or judging. In which kind of life, or as I may terme it, Prentiship, what action or object soever presents it-selfe into our eies, may serve us in stead of a sufficient booke. A prettie pranke of a boy, a knavish tricke of a page, a foolish part of a lackey, an idle tale or any discourse else, spoken either in jest or earnest, at the table or in companie, are even as new subjects for us to worke upon : for furtherance whereof, commerce or common societie among men, visiting of forraine countries, and ob-serving of strange fashions, are verie necessary, not only to be able (after the manner of our yong gal-lants of France) to report how many paces the Church of Santa Rotonda is in length or breadth, or what rich garments the curtezan Signora Livia wear-eth, and the worth of her hosen ; or as some do, nicely to dispute how much longer or broader the face of Nero is, which they have seene in some old ruines of Italie, than that which is made for him in other old monuments else-where. But they should principally observe, and be able to make certaine relation of the humours and fashions of those coun-tries they have seene, that they may the better know how to correct and prepare their wits by those of others. I would therefore have him begin even from his infancie to travell abroad ; and first, that at one shoot he may hit two markes, he should see neighbour-countries, namely where languages are most different from ours ; for, unlesse a mans tongue be fashioned unto them in his youth, he shall never attaine to the true pronunciation of them if he once grow in yeares. Moreover, we see it received as a common opinion of the wiser sort, that it agreeth not with reason, that a childe be alwaies nuzzled, cockered, dandled, and brought up in his parents lap or sight ; forsomuch as their naturall kindnesse, or (as I may call it) tender fondnesse, causeth often, even the wisest to prove so idle, so overnice, and so base-minded. For parents are not capable, neither can they find in their hearts to see them checkt, corrected, or chastised, nor indure to see them brought up so meanly, and so far from daintinesse, and many times so dangerously, as they must needs be. . .

It is not sufficient to make his minde strong, his muskles must also be strengthened : the mind is overborne if it be not seconded : and it is too much for her alone to discharge two offices. I have a feeling how mine panteth, being joyned to so tender and sensible a bodie, and that lieth so heavie upon it. . .

. . . That mind which harboureth Philosophie, ought by reason of her sound health, make that bodie also sound and healthie : it ought to make her contentment to through-shine in all exteriour parts : it ought to shapen and modell all outward demeanours to the modell of it : and by consequence arme him that doth possesse it, with a gracious stoutnesse and lively audacite, with an active and pleasing gesture, and with a setled and cheereful countenance. The most evident token and apparent signe of true wisdome is a constant and unconstrained rejoycing, whose estate is like unto all things above the Moone, that is ever cleare, alwaies bright. . . Shee aymeth at nothing but vertue ; it is vertue shee seekes after ; which as the schoole saith, is not pitcht on the top of an high, steepie, or inaccessible hill ; for they that have come unto her, affirme that cleane-contrarie shee keeps her stand, and holds her mansion in a faire, flourishing, and pleasant plaine, whence as from an high watch tower, she survaieth all things, to be subject unto her, to whom any man may with great facilitie come, if he but know the way or entrance to her palace : for, the pathes that lead unto her are certaine fresh and shadie greene allies, sweet and flowrie waies, whose ascent is even, easie, and nothing wearisome, like unto that of heavens vaults. Forsomuch as they have not frequented this vertue, who gloriously, as in a throne of Majestie, sits soveraigne, goodly, triumphant, lovely, equally delicious, and couragious, protesting her selfe to be a professed and irreconcileable enemie to all sharpnesse, austerite, feare, and compulsion ; having nature for her guide, fortune and volptuousnesse for her companions. . .

She knoweth the way how to be rich, mightie and wise, and how to lie in sweet-perfumed beds. She loveth life ; she delights in beautie, in glorie, and in health. But her proper and particular office is, first to know how to use such goods temperately, and how to lose them constantly. . .

Yet would I not have this young gentleman pent-up, nor carelessly cast-off to the heedlesse choler, or melancholy humour of the hasty Schoolemaster. I would not have his budding spirit corrupted with keeping him fast-tied, and as it were labouring fourteene or fifteene houres a day poaring on his booke, as some doe, as if he were a daylabouring man ; neither doe I thinke it fit, if at any time, by reason of some solitairie or melancholy complexion, he should be seene with an over-indiscreet application given to his booke, it should be cherished in him ; for, that doth often make him both unapt for civill conversation and distracts him

from better imployments : How many have I seene
in my daies, by an over-greedy desire of knowledge,
become as it were foolish ? . . .

. . . All sports and exercises shall be a part of his
study ; running, wrestling, musicke, dancing, hunting, and managing of armes and horses. I would
have the exterior demeanor or decencie, and the disposition of his person to be fashioned together with
his mind : for, it is not a mind, it is not a body that
we erect, but it is a man, and we must not make two
parts of him. . .

. . . The bodie being yet souple, ought to be accommodated to all fashions and customes ; and (alwaies provided, his appetites and desires be kept under) let a yong man boldly be made fit for al Nations and companies ; yea, if need be, for al disorders and surfetings ; let him acquaint him selfe
with al fashions ; That he may be able to do al
things, and love to do none but those that are commendable. . .

How wide are they, which go about to allure a
childs mind to go to its booke, being yet but tender
and fearefull, with a stearne-frowning countenance,
and with hands full of rods ? . . . How much more
decent were it to see their school-houses and formes
strewed with greene boughs and flowers, than with
bloudy burchen-twigs ? If it lay in me, I would doe
as the Philosopher Speusippus did, who caused the
pictures of Gladness and Joy, of Flora and of the
Graces, to be set up round about his school-house.
Where their profit lieth, there should also be their
recreation. Those meats ought to be sugred over,
that are healthful for childrens stomakes, and those
made bitter that are hurtfull for them. . .

Montaigne's own education

I must needs acknowledge, that the Greeke and Latine tongues are great ornaments in a gentleman, but they are purchased at over-high a rate. Use it who list, I will tell you how they may be gotten better, cheaper, and much sooner than is ordinarily used, which was tried in myselfe. My late father, having, by all the meanes and industrie that is possible for a man, sought amongst the wisest, and men of best understanding, to find a most exquisite and readie way of teaching, being advised of the inconveniences then in use ; was given to understand that the lingring while, and best part of our youth, that we imploy in learning the tongues, which cost them nothing, is the onely cause we can never attaine to that absolute perfection of skill and knowledge of the Greekes and Romanes. I doe not beleeve that to be the onely cause. But so it is, the expedient my father found out was this ; that being yet at nurse, and before the first loosing of my tongue, I was delivered to a Germaine (who died since, a most excellent Physitian in France) he being then altogether ignorant of the French tongue, but exquisitely readie and skilfull in the Latine. This man, whom my father had sent for of purpose, and to whom he gave verie great entertainment, had me continually in his armes, and was mine onely overseer. There were also joyned unto him two of his countrimen, but not so learned ; whose charge was to attend, and now and then to play with me ; and all these together did never entertaine me with other than the Latine tongue. As for others of his household, it was an inviolable rule, that neither himselfe, nor my mother, nor man, nor maid-servant, were suffered to speake one word in my companie, except such Latine words as every one had learned to chat and prattle with me. It were strange to tell how every one in the house profited therein. My Father and my Mother learned so much Latine, that for a need they could understand it, when they heard it spoken, even so did all the household servants, namely such as were neerest and most about me. To be short, we were all so Latinized, that the townes round about us had their share of it; insomuch as even at this day, many Latine names both of workmen and of their tooles are yet in use amongst them. And as for myselfe, I was about six years old, and could understand no more French or Perigordine than Arabike; and that without art, without bookes, rules, or grammer, without whipping or whining, I had gotten as pure a Latin tongue as my Master could speake; the rather because I could neither mingle or confound the same with other tongues. . .

As for the Greeke, wherein I have but small understanding, my father purposed to make me learne it by art; But by new and uncustomed meanes, that is, by way of recreation and exercise. We did tosse our declinations and conjugations to and fro, as they doe, who by way of a certaine game at tables learne both Arithmetike and Geometrie. For, amongst other things he had especially beene perswaded to make me taste and apprehend the fruits of dutie and science by an unforced kinde of will, and of mine owne choice; and without any compulsion or rigor to bring me up in all mildnesse and libertie:

yea with such kinde of superstition, that, whereas some are of opinion that suddenly to awaken young children, and as it were by violence to startle and fright them out of their dead sleepe in a morning (wherein they are more heavie and deeper plunged than we) doth greatly trouble and distemper their braines, he would every morning cause me to be awakened by the sound of some instrument; and I was never without a servant who to that purpose attended upon me.

This example may serve to judge of the rest; as also to commend the judgement and tender affection of so carefull and loving a father: who is not to be blamed, though hee reaped not the fruits answerable to his exquisite toyle and painefull manuring. Two things hindered the same; first the barrennesse and unfit soyle: for howbeit I were of a sound and strong constitution, and of a tractable and yeelding condition, yet was I so heavie, so sluggish, and so dull, that I could not be rouzed (yea were it to goe to play) from out mine idle drowzinesse. What I saw, I saw it perfectly; and under this heavy, and as it were Lethe-complexion did I breed hardie imaginations, and opinions farre above my yeares. My spirit was very slow, and would goe no further, than it was led by others; my apprehension blockish, my invention poore; and besides, I had a marvelous defect in my weake memorie; it is therefore no wonder, if my father could never bring me to any perfection. . .

Bk. I, ch. 25, *Of the Institution and Education of Children*

Friendship with Etienne de la Boëtie

To compare the affection toward women unto it, although it proceed from our owne free choice, a man cannot, nor may it be placed in this ranke : its fire, I confesse it . . . to be more active, more fervent, and more sharpe. But it is a rash and wavering fire, waving and divers : the fire of an ague subject to fits and stints, and that hath but slender hold-fast of us. In true friendship, it is a generall and universall heat, and equally tempered, a constant and setled heat, all pleasure and smoothness that hath no pricking or stinging in it, which the more it is in lustfull love, the more is it but a raging and mad desire in following that which flies us. . .

Those we ordinarily call friendes and amities, are but acquaintances and familiarities, tied together by some occasion or commodities, by meanes whereof our mindes are entertained. In the amitie I speake of, they enter-mixe and confound themselves one in the other, with so universall a commixture, that they weare out and can no more finde the seame that hath conjoined them together. If a man urge me to tell wherefore I loved him, I feele it cannot be expressed, but by answering ; Because it was he, because it was my selfe. There is beyond all my discourse, and besides what I can particularly report of it, I know not what inexplicable and fatall power, a meane and Mediatrix of this indissoluble union. We sought one another before we had seene one another, and by the reports we heard one of another ; which wrought a greater violence in us, than the reason of reports may well beare ; I thinke by some secret ordinance of the heavens, we embraced one another by our names.   And at our first meeting, which was by chance at a great feast, and solemne meeting of a whole towneship, we found our selves so surprized, so knowne, so acquainted, and so combinedly bound together, that from thence forward, nothing was so neer unto us as one unto another. . . Since the time I lost him . . .

I doe but languish, I doe but sorrow : and even those pleasures, all things present me with, in stead of yeelding me comfort, doe but redouble the griefe of his losse.   We were copartners in all things.   All things were with us at halfe ; me thinkes I have stolne his part from him.

I was so accustomed to be ever two, and so enured to be never single, that me thinks I am but halfe my selfe.

Bk. I, ch. 27, *Of Friendship*

Report of New World

. . . I have had long time dwelling with me a man, who for the space of ten or twelve yeares had dwelt in that other world, which in our age was lately discovered in those parts where Villegaignon first landed, and surnamed Antartike France.   This discoverie of so infinit and vast a countrie, seemeth worthy great consideration.   I wot not whether I can warrant my selfe, that some other be not discovered hereafter, sithence so many worthy men, and better learned than we are, have so many ages beene deceived in this. . .

This servant I had, was a simple and rough-hewen fellow : a condition fit to yeeld a true testimonie. For, subtile people may indeed marke more curiously, and observe things more exactly, but they amplifie and glose them : and the better to perswade, and make their interpretations of more validitie, they cannot chuse but somewhat alter the storie. They never represent things truly, but fashion and maske them according to the visage they saw them in ; and to purchase credit to their judgement, and draw you on to beleeve them, they commonly adorne, enlarge, yea, and hyperbolize the matter. Wherein is required either a most sincere Reporter, or a man so simple, that he may have no invention to build upon and to give a true likelihood unto false devices, and be not wedded to his owne will. Such a one was my man . . .

I would have every man write what he knowes, and no more : not only in that, but in all other subjects. For one may have particular knowledge of the nature of one river, and experience of the qualitie of one fountaine, that in other things knowes no more than another man : who neverthelesse to publish this little scantling, will undertake to write of all the Physickes. From which vice proceed divers great inconveniences. Now (to returne to my purpose) I finde (as farre as I have beene informed) there is nothing in that nation that is either barbarous or savage, unless men call that barbarisme which is not common to them. As indeed, we have no other ayme of truth and reason, than the example and Idea of the opinions and customes of the countrie we live in. It is ever perfect religion, perfect policie, perfect and compleat use of all things. . .

It is a nation, . . . that hath no kinde of traffike, no knowledge of Letters, no intelligence of num-

bers, no name of magistrate, nor of politike superi-
oritie ; no use of service, of riches or of povertie ;
no contracts, no successions, no partitions, no occupation but idle ; no respect of kindred, but common,
no apparell but naturall, no manuring of lands, no
use of wine, corne, or mettle.   The very words that
import lying, falsehood, treason, dissimulations, cov-
etousnes, envie, detraction, and pardon, were never
heard of amongst them. . .

All this is not verie ill ; but what of that ?   They
weare no kinde of breeches nor hosen.

Bk. I, ch. 30, Of Caniballes

Poetry

Loe, here are wonders, we have more Poets than
judges and interpreters of poesie.   It is an easier
matter to frame it than to know it : Being base and
humble, it may be judged by the precepts and art
of it : But the good and loftie, the supreme and
divine, is beyond rules and above reason.   Whosoever discerneth her beautie, with a constant, quicke-
seeing, and setled looke, he can no more see and
comprehend the same than the splendor of a lightning flash.   It hath no communitie with our judgement ; but ransacketh and ravisheth the same.   The
furie which prickes and moves him that can penetrate her, doth also stricke and wound a third man,
if he heare it either handled or recited, as the ada-
mant stone drawes not only a needle, but infuseth
some of her facultie in the same to draw others :
And it is more apparently seene in theaters, that the
sacred inspiration of the Muses, having first stirred

up the Poet with a kinde of agitation unto choler, unto griefe, unto hatred, yea and beyond himselfe, whither and howsoever they please, doth also by the Poet strike and enter into the Actor, and consequently by the Actor a whole auditorie or multitude. It is the ligament of our senses depending one of another. Even from my infancie Poesie hath had the vertue to transpierce and transport me.

Bk. I, ch. 36, Of Cato the Younger

How he composes his book

Judgement is an instrument for all subjects, and medleth every where, and therefore the Essayes I make of it, there is no maner of occasion I seeke not to employ therein. If it be a subject I understand not my selfe, therein I make triall of it, sounding afarre off the depth of the ford, and finding the same over deepe for my reach, I keepe my selfe on the shoare. And to acknowledge not to be able to wade through is a part of its effect, yea of such whereof it vanteth most. If I light upon a vaine and idle subject, I assay to trie and endevour to see whether it may find a good ground to worke upon, and matter to give it body, and wherewith to support and under-lay it. Sometimes I addresse my judgement and contrive it to a noble and out-worne subject, wherein it can find nothing of itselfe, the high way to it being so bare-trodden that it cannot march but in others' steps. There it pleaseth itselfe in chusing the course it thinkes best, and of a thousand paths sometimes it saith, this or that was best chosen. I take my first Argument of fortune : all are alike unto me ; and I never purpose to handle them throughly. . . Of a hundred parts and visages that every thing hath, I take one, which sometimes I slightly runne over, and other times but cursorily glance at. And yet other whilse I pinch it to the quicke and give it a Stockado, not the widest, but the deepest I can. And for the most part I love to seize upon them by some unwonted lustre. I would adventure to treat and discourse of some matter to the depth, knew I my selfe lesse, or were I deceived in mine owne impuissance ; scattering here one and there another word, scantlings taken from their maine groundwork, disorderly dispersed, without any well-grounded designe and promise. I am not bound to make it good, nor without varying to keepe my selfe close-tied unto it ; whensoever it shall please me to yeeld my selfe to doubt, to uncertaintie, and to my mistress's forme, which is ignorance. Each motion sheweth and discovereth what we are.

Bk. I, ch. 50, *Of Democritus & Heraclitus*

If these Essayes were worthy to be judged of, it might in mine opinion happen that they would not greatly please the common and vulgar spirits, and as little the singular and excellent. The first will understand but little of them, the latter over much ; they might perhaps live and rub out in the middle region.

Bk. I, ch. 54, *Of Vaine subtilities or subtill Devices*

Man's mobility

. . . There is nothing I so hardly beleeve to be
in man as constancie, and nothing so easie to be
found in him, as inconstancy. . .

Our ordinary manner is to follow the inclination
of our appetite this way and that way, on the left
and on the right hand ; upward and downeward, according as the winde of occasions doth transport us :
we never thinke on what we would have, but at the
instant we would have it : and change as that beast
that takes the colour of the place wherein it is laid.
What we even now purposed we alter by and by,
and presently returne to our former biase : all is but
changing, motion, and inconstancy . . .

We goe not, but we are carried : as things that
flote, now gliding gently, now hulling violently, according as the water is either stormy or calme.

Every day new toyes, each hour new fantasies,
and our humours move and fleet with the fleetings
and movings of time. . . And whosoever shall heed-
fully survey and consider himselfe, shall finde this
volubility and discordance to be in himselfe, yea
and in his very judgement. I have nothing to say
entirely, simply, and with soliditie of my selfe,
without confusion, disorder, blending, mingling, nor
in one word. Distinguo is the most universall part
of my logike. . . Therefore to judge a man, we
must a long time follow, and very curiously marke
his steps. . .

It is no part of a well-grounded judgement simply
to judge ourselves by our exteriour actions : A man
must thorowly sound himselfe, and dive into his
heart, and there see by what wards or springs the

motions stirre. But forsomuch as it is a hazardous
and high enterprise, I would not have so many to
meddle with it as doe.

Bk. II, ch. 1, *Of the Inconstancie of our Actions*

His Father

. . . His demeanour and carriage was ever milde,
meeke, gentle, and very modest, and above all grave
and stately. There is nothing he seemed to be more
carefull of than of his honesty, and observe a kinde
of decencie of his person, and orderly decorum in
his habits, were it on foot or on horsebacke. He
was exceeding nice in performing his word or promise. And so strictly conscientious and obsequious
in religion, that generally he seemed rather to
encline toward superstition than the contrarie.
Though he were but a little man, his courage and
vigor was great. He was of an upright and well
proportioned stature, of a pleasing, cheerfull-looking
countenance, of a swarthy hue, nimbly addicted,
and exquisitely nimble unto all noble and gentleman-
like exercises. I have seene some hollow staves of
his filled with lead which hee wont to use and exercise his armes withall, the better to enable himselfe
to pitch the barre, to throw the sledge, to cast the
pole, and to play at fence ; and shoes with leaden
soles, which he wore to ensure himselfe to leape, to
vault, and to run. I may without blushing say, that
in memorie of himselfe, he hath left certaine petie
miracles amongst us. I have seene him when he was
past threescore years of age mocke at all our sports,
and out-countenance our youthfull pastimes, with
a heavy furr'd gowne about him to leape into his

saddle, to make the pommada round about a table upon his thumb, and seldome to ascend any staires without skipping three or four steps at once. . .

Bk. II, ch. 2, Of Drunkennesse

His Accident

It is a hard matter (although our conceit doe willingly apply it selfe unto it) that Discourse and Instruction should sufficiently be powerful to direct us to action, and addresse us to performance, if, over and besides that, we doe not by experience exercise and frame our minde to the traine whereunto we will range it. . .

But to dye, which is the greatest worke we have to doe, exercise can nothing availe us thereunto. A man may, by custome and experience, fortifie himselfe against griefe, sorrow, shame, want, and such like accidents ; but concerning death, we can but once feele and trie the same. We are all novices, and new to learne when we come unto it. . .

Me seemeth, neverthelesse, that in some sort there is a meane to familiarize our selves with it, and to assay it. We may have some experience of it, if not whole and perfect, at least such as may not altogether be unprofitable, and which may yeeld us better fortified and more assured. If we cannot attaine unto it, we may at least approch it, and discerne the same : And if we cannot enter her fort, yet shal we see and frequent the approches unto it. It is not without reason we are taught to take notice of our sleepe for the resemblance it hath with death. How easily we passe from waking to sleeping ; with how little interest we lose the knowledge of light and of our selves. . .

But such as by some violent accident are falne into a faintnes of heart, and have lost all senses, they, in mine opinion, have well-nigh beene where they might behold her true and naturall visage : For, touching the instant or moment of the passage, it is not to be feared it should bring any traveil or dis-pleasure with it, forasmuch as we can have nor sense nor feeling without leasure. Our sufferances have need of time, which is so short, and plunged in death, that necessarily it must be insensible. It is the ap-proches that lead unto it we should feare ; and those may fall within the compasse of mans experience. Many things seeme greater by imagination than by effect. I have passed over a good part of my age in sound and perfect health. I say, not only sound, but blithe and wantonly-lustfull. That state full of lust, of prime and mirth, made me deeme the consideration of sicknesses so yrkesome and horrible, that when I came to the experience of them, I have found their fits but weake, and their assaults but faint, in respect of my apprehended feare. Lo here what I daily prove. Let me be under a roofe, in a good chamber, warme-clad, and well at ease, in some tempestuous and stormy night. I am exceedingly perplexed and much grieved for such as are abroad and have no shelter : But let me be in the storme my selfe, I doe not so much as desire to be else-where. . .

During our second or third troubles (I doe not well remember which) I fortuned one day, for recreation sake, to goe forth and take the ayre, about

a league from my house, who am seated even in the
bowels of all troubles of our civill warres of France,
supposing to be most safe, so neere mine owne home
and retreite, that I had no need of better attendance
or equipage. I was mounted upon a very easie-
going nag, but not very sure. At my returning
home againe, a sudden occasion being offered me to
make use of this nag in a peece of service whereto
he was neither trained nor accustomed, one of my
men (a strong sturdy fellow), mounted upon a
young strong-headed horse, and that a desperate
hard mouth, fresh, lusty and in breath, to shew his
courage, and to outgoe his fellowes, fortuned with
might and maine to set spurres unto him, and giving
him the bridle, to come right into the path where I
was, and as a Colossus with his weight riding over
me and my nag, that were both very little, he over-
threw us both, and made us fall with our heeles upward : so that the nag lay along astonied in one
place, and I in a trance groveling on the ground
ten or twelfe paces wide of him : my face all torne
and brused, my sword which I had in my hand a
good way from me, my girdle broken, with no more
motion or sense in me than a stocke. It is the only
swooning that ever I felt yet. Those that were
with me, after they had assayed all possible meanes
to bring me to my selfe againe, supposing me dead,
tooke me in their armes, and with much adoe were
carrying me home to my house, which was about
halfe a French league thence : upon the way, and
after I had for two houres space by all beene supposed dead and past all recoverie, I began to stir
and breathe : for so great aboundance of bloud was
falne into my stomake, that to discharge it nature

was forced to rowse up her spirits. I was immediately set upon my feet, and bending forward, I presently cast up in quantitie as much clottie pure bloud as a bucket will hold, and by the way was constrained to doe the like divers times before I could get home, whereby I began to recover a little life, but it was by little and little, and so long adoing, that my chiefe senses were much more enclining to death than to life.

The remembrance whereof (which yet I beare deeply imprinted in my minde) representing me her visage and Idea so lively and so naturally doth in some sort reconcile me unto her. And when I began to see, it was with so dim, so weake and so troubled a sight, that I could not discerne anything of the light. . .

Touching the functions of the soule, they started up and came in the same progresse as those of the bodie. I perceived my selfe all bloudy; for my doublet was all sullied with the bloud I had cast. The first conceit I apprehended was that I had received some shot in my head; and in truth, at the same instant, there were divers that shot round about us. Me thought my selfe had no other hold of me but of my lips-ends. I closed mine eyes to help (as me seemed) to send it forth, and tooke a kinde of pleasure to linger and languishingly to let my selfe goe from my selfe. It was an imagination swimming superficially in my minde, as weake and as tender as all the rest: but in truth, not only exempted from displeasure, but rather commixt with that pleasant sweetnesse which they feel that suffer themselves to fall into a soft-slumbring and sense-entrancing sleepe. I beleeve it is the same state they find themselves in, whom in the agony of death we see to droop and faint thorow weaknesse : and am of opinion we plaine and moane them without cause, esteeming that either they are agitated with grievous pangs, or that their soule is pressed with painfull cogitations. . .

When I came neere my house, where the tidings of my fall was already come, and those of my household met me, with such outcries as are used in like times, I did not only answer some words to what I was demanded, but some tell me I had the memory to command my men to give my wife a horse, whom I perceived to be over-tired, and labouring in the way, which is very hilly, foule, and rugged. It seemeth this consideration proceeded from a vigilant soule : yet was I cleane distracted from it, they were but vaine conceits, and as in a cloud, only moved by the sense of the eyes and eares : They came not from my selfe. All which notwithstanding, I knew neither whence I came nor whither I went, nor could I understand or consider what was spoken unto me. They were but light effects, that my senses produced of themselves, as it were of custome. Whatsoever the soule did assist it with was but a dreame, being lightly touched, and only sprinkled by the soft impression of the senses. In the meane time my state was verily most pleasant and easefull. I felt no manner of care or affliction, neither for my selfe nor others. It was a slumbering, languishing and extreme weaknesse, without any paine at all. I saw mine own house and knew it not ; when I was laid in my bed, I felt great ease in my rest, For I had beene vilely hurried and haled by those poore men, which had taken the paines to carry me upon their armes a long and wearysome way, and to say truth, they had all beene wearied twice or thrice over, and were faine to shift severall times. Many remedies were presently offered me, but I tooke none, supposing verily I had beene deadly hurt in the head. To say truth, it had beene a very happy death : For, the weaknesse of my discourse hindered me from judging of it, and the feeblenesse of my body from feeling the same. Me thought I was yeelding up the ghost so gently, and after so easie and indolent a manner, that I feele no other action lesse burthensome than that was. But when I began to come to life againe and recover my former strength — which was within two or three houres after, I presently felt my selfe full of aches and paines all my body over ; for, each part thereof was with the violence of the fall much brused and tainted ; and for two or three nights after I found my self so ill, that I verily supposed I shold have had another fit of death : But that a more lively, and sensible one : (and to speak plaine) I feele my bruses yet, and feare me shall do while I live : I will not forget to tell you, that the last thing I could rightly fall into againe was the remembrance of this accident, and I made my men many times to repeat me over and over againe, whither I was going, whence I came, and what houre that chance befell me, before I could throughly conceive it. Concerning the manner of my falling, they in favour of him who had beene the cause of it, concealed the truth from me, and told me other flim flam tales. But a while after and the morrow next, when my memorie began to come to itselfe againe, and represent the state unto me wherein I was at the instant, when I perceived the horse riding over me (for being at my heeles, I chanced to espy him and helde my selfe for dead : yet was the conceit so sudden that feare had no leasure to enter my thoughts) me seemed it was a flashing or lightning that smote my soule with shaking, and that I came from another world. . .

Bk. II, ch. 6, *Of Exercise or Practice*

Difficulty of Self-study

It is a thorny and crabbed enterprise, and more than it makes show of, to follow so strange and vagabond a path as that of our spirit : to penetrate the shady, and enter the thicke-covered depths of these internall winding crankes ; to chuse so many and settle so severall aires of its agitations ; and tis a new extraordinary amusement that distracts us from the common occupation of the world, yea, and from the most recommended. Many yeares are past since I have no other aime whereto my thoughts bend, but my selfe, and that I controule and study nothing but my selfe. And if I study anything else, it is immediately to place it upon, or, to say better, in my selfe. And me thinkes I err not if, as commonly men doe in other sciences, without all comparison less profitable, I impart what I have learn't by this, although I greatly content not my selfe with the progresse I have made therein. There is no description so hard, nor assuredly so profitable, as is the description of a mans own self. . .

Bk. II, ch. 6, *Of Exercise or Practice*

Treatment of children

Now if we shall duly consider this simple occasion of loving our children, because we have begotten them, for which we call them our other selves ; it seemes there is another production coming from us, and which is of no lesse recommendation and consequence. For what we engender by the minde, the fruits of our courage, sufficiencie, or spirit, are brought forth by a far more noble part than the corporall, and more our owne.   We are both father and mother together in this generation ; such fruits cost us much dearer and bring us more honour, and chiefly if they have any good or rare thing in them. For the value of our other children is much more theirs than ours.   The share we have in them is but little, but of these all the beautie, all the grace, and all the worth is ours. . .

I utterly condemne all manner of violence in the education of a young spirit, brought up to honour and libertie.   There is a kind of slavishnesse in churlish rigour, and servility in compulsion ; and I hold that that which cannot be compassed by reason, wisdome, and discretion, can never be attained by force and constraint.   So was I brought up : they tell me that in all my youth I never felt rod but twice, and that very lightly.   And what education I have had myselfe, the same have I given my children. . .

The Lord of Montluc, late one of the Lord Marshals of France, having lost his sonne, who died in the Iland of Madera, a worthy, forward and gallant young gentleman, and truely of good hope, amongst

other his griefes and regrets did greatly move me
to condole the infinite displeasure and hearts-sorrow
that he felt, inasmuch as he had never communi-
cated and opened himselfe vnto him : for, with his
austere humour and continuall endevouring to hold
a grimme-stern-fatherly gravity over him, he had
lost the meanes perfectly to finde and throughly to
know his sonne, and so to manifest vnto him the extreme affection he bare him, and the worthy judgement he made of his vertue. 'Alas,' was he wont
to say, 'the poore lad saw never anything in me but
a severe-surly countenance, full of disdaine, and
haply was possessed with this conceit, that I could
neither love nor esteeme him according to his merits.
Ay-me, to whom did I reserve, to discover that
singular and loving affection which in my soule I
bare vnto him ? Was it not he that should have
had all the pleasure and acknowledgement thereof ?
I have forced and tormented my selfe to maintaine
this vaine maske, and have vtterly lost the pleasure
of his conversation, and therwithal his good will,
which surely was but faintly cold towards me, forsomuch as he never received but rude entertainement
of me, and never felt but a tyrannicall proceeding
in me towards him.' I am of opinion his complaint
was reasonable and well grounded. For, as I know
by certaine experience, there is no comfort so sweet
in the losse of friends, as that our owne knowledge
or conscience tels vs we never omitted to tell them
everything, and expostulate all matters vnto them,
and to have had a perfect and free communication
with them.

Bk. II, ch. 8, *Of the Affection of Fathers to their Children*

Reading

I make no doubt but it shall often befall me to speake of things which are better, and with more truth, handled by such as are their crafts-masters. Here is simply an essay of my natural faculties, and no whit of those I have acquired. And he that shall tax me with ignorance shall have no great victory at my hands ; for hardly could I give others reasons for my discourses that give none unto my selfe, and am not well satisfied with them. He that shall make search after knowledge, let him seek it where it is : there is nothing I professe lesse. These are but my fantasies by which I endevour not to make things known, but my selfe. They may haply one day be knowne unto me, or have bin at other times, according as fortune hath brought me where they were declared or manifested. But I remember them no more. And if I be a man of some reading, yet I am a man of no remembering . . .

If in reading I fortune to meet with any difficult points, I fret not my selfe about them, but after I have given them a charge or two, I leave them as I found them. Should I earnestly plod upon them, I should loose both time and my selfe, for I have a skipping wit. What I see not at the first view, I shall lesse see it if I opinionate my selfe upon it. I doe nothing without blithnesse ; and an over obstinate continuation and plodding contention doth dazle, dul, and wearie the same : my sight is thereby confounded and diminished. I must therefore withdraw it, and at fittes goe to it againe. If one booke seeme tedious unto me I take another, which I follow not with any earnestnesse, except it be at such houres that I begin to be weary with doing nothing. . .

Knowledge and truth may be in us without judgement, and we may have judgement without them : yea, the acknowledgement of ignorance is one of the best and surest testimonies of judgement that I can finde. I have no other sergeant of band to marshall my rapsodies than fortune. And looke how my humours or conceites present themselves, so I shuffle them up. Sometimes they prease out thicke and three fold, and other times they come out languishing one by one. I will have my naturall and ordinarie pace seene as loose and as shuffling as it is. As I am, so I goe on plodding. . .

Bk. II, ch. 10, *Of Bookes*

Opinion

How diversely judge we of things ? How often change we our phantasies ? What I hold and beleeve this day I beleeve and hold with all my beleefe : all my implements, springs and motions, embrace and claspe this opinion, and to the utmost of their power warrant the same : I could not possibly embrace any verity, nor with more assurance keepe it, than I doe this. I am wholy and absolutely given to it : but hath it not beene my fortune, not once, but a hundred, nay a thousand times, nay daily, to have embraced some other thing with the very same instruments and condition which upon better advise I have afterward judged false ? A man should at the least become wise at his owne cost, and learne by others harmes. If under this colour I have often found my selfe deceived, if my Touchstone be commonly found false and my ballance un-even and unjust; what assurance may I more take of it at this time than at others? Is it not folly in me to suffer my selfe so often to be beguiled and couzened by one guide? Neverthelesse, let fortune remove us five hundred times from our place, let her doe nothing but incessantly empty and fill, as in a vessell, other and other opinions in our mind, the present and last is alwaies supposed certaine and infallible. For this must a man leave goods, honour, life, state, health and all. I that nearest prie into my selfe, and who have mine eyes uncessantly fixt upon me as one that hath not much else to do else where, dare very hardly report the vanity and weaknesse I feele in my selfe. My foot is so staggering and unstable, and I finde it so ready to trip, and so easie to stumble; and my sight is so dimme and uncertaine that fasting I finde my selfe other than full fed. If my health applaud me, or but the calmenesse of one faire day smile upon me, then am I a lusty gallant; but if a corne wring my toe, then am I pouting, unpleasant and hard to be pleased. One same pace of a horse is sometimes hard and sometimes easie unto me; and one same way, one time short, another time long and weari-some; and one same forme, now more, now lesse agreeable and pleasing to mee: sometimes I am apt to doe any thing, and other times fit to doe nothing: what now is pleasing to me within a while after will be painefull. There are a thousand indiscreet and casuall agitations in me. Either a melancholy hu-mour possesseth me, or a cholericke passion swaieth me, which having shaken off, sometimes froward-nesse and peevishnesse hath predominancy, and other times gladnes and blithnesse overrule me. If I chance to take a booke in hand I shall in some passages perceive some excellent graces, and which ever wound me to the soule with delight; but let me lay it by and read him another time; let me turne and tosse him as I list, let me apply and manage him as I will, I shall finde it an unknowne and shapelesse masse. Even in my writings I shall not at all times finde the tracke or ayre of my first imaginations; I wot not my selfe what I would have said, and shall vexe and fret my selfe in correcting and giving a new sense to them, because I have peradventure forgotten or lost the former, which happily was better. I doe but come and goe; my judgement doth not alwaies goe forward, but is ever floting and wandering.

Many times (as commonly it is my hap to doe) having for exercise and sport-sake undertaken to maintaine an opinion contrarie to mine, my minde applying and turning it selfe that way doth so tie me unto it, as I finde no more the reason of my former conceit, and so I leave it. Where I encline, there I entertaine my selfe howsoever it be, and am carried away by mine owne weight. Every man could neer-hand say as much of himselfe would he but looke into himselfe as I doe. . .

Que sçais-je

In few, there is no constant existence, neither of our being, nor of the objects. And we and our judgement and all mortall things else do uncessantly rowle, turne and passe away. Thus can nothing be certainely established, nor of the one nor of the other ; both the judgeing and the judged being in continuall alteration and motion. We have no communication with being ; for every humane nature is ever in the middle betweene being borne and dying ; giving nothing of it selfe but an obscure apparence and shadow, and an uncertaine and weake opinion. And if perhaps you fix your thought to take its being, it would be even as if one should go about to graspe the water : for, how much the more he shal close and presse that which by its owne nature is ever gliding, so much the more he shall loose what he would hold and fasten. Thus, seeing all things are subject to passe from one change to another, reason, which therein seeketh a reall subsistence, findes her selfe deceived as unable to apprehend any thing subsistent and permanent : forsomuch as each thing either commeth to a being, and is not yet altogether : or beginneth to dy before it be borne.

Bk. II, ch. 12, *An Apologie of Raymond Sebond*

His house undefended during the Civil Wars

'Things sealed up solicite a thief to break them open : Whereas a common burglayer will passe by quietly things that lie open.' Amongst other meanes, ease and facility doth haply cover and fence my house from the violence of civill wares : Inclosure and fencing drawe on enterprise, and distrust, offence. I have abated and weakened the souldiers designe by taking hazard and all means of military glory from their exploite, which is wont to serve them for a title, and stead them for an excuse. What is performed couragiously, at what time justice lieth dead, is ever done honourably. I yeeld them the conquest of my house dastardly and treacherous. It is never shut to any that knocketh. It hath no other guardian or provision but a porter, as an ancient custome, and used ceremony, who serveth not so much to defend my gate as to offer it more decently and courteously to all comers. I have nor watch nor sentinell but what the starres keepe for mee. That gentleman is much to blame who makes a shew to stand upon his guarde, except he be very strong indeed. Who so is open on one side is so every where. Our fore-fathers never dreamed on building of frontire townes and castles.

The meanes to assaile (I meane without battery and troopes of armed men) and to surprise our houses, encrease daily beyond the meanes of garding or defending. Mens wits are generally exasperated and whetted on that way. Invasion concerneth all, defence none but the rich. Mine was sufficiently strong, according to the times when it was made. I have since added nothing unto it that way ; and I would feare the strength of it should turne against my selfe. Seeing a peaceable time will require we shall unfortifie them. It is dangerous not to be able to recover them againe, and it is hard for one to be assured of them. For concerning intestine broils, your owne servant may be of that faction you stand in feare of. And where religion serveth for a pretence, even alliances and consanguinitie become mistrustful under colour of justice. Public finances cannot entertaine our private garrisons. They should all be consumed. We have not wherewith, nor are wee able to doe it without our ruine, or more incommodiously and therewithall injuriously, with-

out the common peoples destruction. . . That
so many strongly-garded houses have been lost,
whereas mine continueth still, makes me suspect
they were overthrowne onely because they were so
diligently garded. It is that which affoordeth a
desire and ministreth a pretence to the assailant.
All gards beare a shew of warre, which if God be
so pleased may light upon me. But so it is, I will
never call for it. It is my sanctuary or retreate to
rest my selfe from warres. I endeavour to free this
corner from the publike storme, as I doe another
corner in my soule. Our warre may change forme
and multiply and diversifie how and as long as it
list, but for my selfe I never stirre. Amongst so
many barricaded and armed houses, none but my
selfe (as farre as I know) of my qualitie hath merely
trusted the protection of his unto the heavens : for
I never removed neither plate, nor hangings, nor my
title-deeds. I will neither feare nor save my selfe by
halfes. If a full acknowledgement purchaseth the
favour of God, it shall last me for ever unto the
end : if not, I have continued long enough to make
my continuance remarkeable and worthy the reg-
istring. What, is not thirtie yeares a goodly time ?

Bk. II, ch. 15, *That our Desires are increased by Difficultie*

His manner of writing and speaking

For in truth, touching the effects of the spirit in
what manner soever, there never came any thing
from me that contented me. And others approbation is no currant payment for me. My judgement
is tender and hard, especially in mine owne behalf.
I feele my self to waver and bend through weak-

nesse : I have nothing of mine owne to satisfie my judgement. My sight is indifferently cleare and regular ; but if I take any serious worke in hand, it is troubled and dimmed : as I perceive most evidently in poesie : I love it exceedingly : I have some insight or knowledge in other mens labours, but in truth I play the novice when I set my hand unto it : then can I not abide my selfe. A man may play the foole every where else, but not in poesie. . .

I have ever an idea in my mind which presents me with a better forme than that I have alreadie framed ; but I can neither lay hold on it nor effect it. Yet is that idea but of the meaner stamp. I thereby conclude that the productions of those rich and great mindes of former ages are farre beyond the extreame extention of my wish and imagination. Their compositions doe not only satisfie and fill me, but they astonish and wrap me into admiration. I judge of their beauty, I see it, if not to the end, at least so farre as it is impossible for me to aspire unto it. Whatsoever I undertake (as Plutarke saith of one) I owe a sacrifice to the Graces, hoping thereby to gaine their favour.

They altogether forsake me : what I doe, it is but bunglingly, and wants both polishing and beauty. . . My workmanship addeth no grace unto the matter. And that's the reason I must have it strong, with good holdfast, and shining of it selfe. . . As for the rest, my language hath neither facility nor fluency in it, but is harsh and sharpe, having free and unsinnowy dispositions. And so it liketh me, if not by my judgement, yet by my inclination. But yet I perceive that sometimes I wade too farre into it,

and that forcing my selfe to avoide art and affectation, I fall into it another way. . .

Beauty

Beauty is a part of great commendation in the
commerce and societie of men. It is the chiefe
meane of reconciliation betweene one and other.
Nor is there any man so barbarous and so hard-
hearted, that in some sort feeleth not himselfe
strucken with her sweetnes. The body hath a
great part in our being, and therein keepes a speciall rancke. For his structure and composition
are worthy due consideration. Such as goe about
to sunder our two principall parts, are much to
blame ; they ought rather to be coupled and joyned
fast together. The soule must be enjoyned not to
retire to her selfe her quarter, nor to entertaine her
selfe apart, nor to despise and leave the body (which
she cannot well doe, except it be by some counter-
faited, apish tricke) but ought so combine and
cling fast unto him, to embrace, to cherish, assist,
correct, perswade, and advise him, and if hee chance
to sway or stray, then to leade and direct him : In
fine, she should wed and serve him as a true husband, that so their effects may not seeme contrary
and divers, but agreeing and uniforme. Christians
have a particular instruction concerning this bond,
for they know that Gods justice alloweth this society, and embraceth this conjunction of the body
and soule, yea so farre as to make the body capable
of everlasting rewards. And that God beholds the
whole man to worke, and will have him entirely to

receive either the punishment or the recompense, according to his demerits. The Peripatetike Sect (of all Sects the most sociable) attributeth this onely care unto wisdome, in common to procure and provide the good of these two associated parts : and declareth other sects to have partialized overmuch, because they had not given themselves to the full consideration of this commixture ; this one for the body, this other for the soule, with one like error and oversight, and had mistaken their subject, which is man ; and their guide, which in generall they avouched to be Nature. The first distinction that hath beene amongst men, and the first consideration that gave preheminence to some over others, it is very likely it was the advantage of beauty.

His physical qualities

My health is blith and lustie, though well-stroken in age, seldome troubled with diseases : Such I was, for I am now engaged in the approaches of age, having long since past over forty yeares.

What hereafter I shall be will be but half a being. I shall be no more my selfe. I daily escape, and still steale my selfe from my selfe.

Of addressing, dexteritie, and disposition, I never had any, yet am I the son of a well disposed father, and of so blithe and merry a disposition, that it continued with him even to his extreamest age. He seldome found any man of his condition, and that could match him in all exercises of the body ; as I have found few that have not out-gone me, except it were in running, wherein I was of the middle sort. As for musicke, were it either in voice, which I have

most harsh, and very unapt, or in instruments, I
could never be taught any part of it. As for dancing, playing at tennis, or wrestling, I could never
attaine to any indifferent sufficiencie, but none at all
in swimming, in fencing, in vaulting, or in leaping.
My hands are so stiffe and nummie, that I can hardly
write for my selfe, so that what I have once scribled,
I had rather frame it a new than take the paines to
correct it ; and I reade but little better. I perceive
how the auditorie censureth me ; otherwise I am no
bad clarke. I cannot very wel close up a letter,
nor could I ever make a pen. I was never good
carver at the table. I could never make readie nor
arme a horse ; nor handsomely array a hawke upon
my fist, nor cast her off, or let her flie, nor could I
ever speake to dogges, to birds, or to horses. The
conditions of my body are, in fine, very well agreeing with those of my minde, wherein is nothing
lively, but onely a compleate and constant vigor. I
endure labour and paine, yet not very well, unlesse
I carry myselfe unto it, and no longer than my desire leadeth and directeth me.

Otherwise, if by any pleasure I be not allured, and
if I have other direction than my genuine and free
will, I am nothing worth ; for I am at such a stay,
that except for health and life, there is nothing I will
take the paines to fret my selfe about, or will purchase at so high a rate as to trouble my wits for it,
or be constrained thereunto. . . I have a minde free
and altogether her owne ; accustomed to follow her
owne humor. And to this day never had, nor commanding, nor forced master. I have gon as farre,
and kept what pace pleased me best : which hath
enfeebled and made me unprofitable to serve others,

and made me fit and apt, but onely for my selfe.
Fewe passions have troubled my sleepe, but of de-
liberations the least doth trouble it. Even as of
high-waies, I willingly seeke to avoid the downe-
hanging and slippery, and take the beaten-path,
though myrie and deepe, so I may go no lower, and
there seeke I safetie.

Falseness

For touching this new-found vertue of faining
and dissimulation, which now is so much in credit, I
hate it to the death : and of all vices I finde none
that so much witnesseth demissenesse and basenesse
of heart. It is a coward and servile humour for a
man to disguise and hide himselfe under a maske, and
not dare to shew himselfe as he is. Thereby our
men address themselves to trecherie : being trained
to utter false words, they make no conscience to
breake them. A generous minde ought not to belie
his thoughts, but make shew of his inmost parts :
there all is good, or at least all is humane. Aristotle
thinkes it an office of magnanimitie to hate and love
openly, to judge and speake with all libertie, and
never at the cost of truth to make esteeme either
of the approbation or reprobation of others. Apol-
lonius said it was for servants to lie, and for free-
men to speake truth. It is the chiefe and fundamentall part of vertue. Shee must be loved for her
owne sake. He that speaketh truth because he is
bound to doe so, and for that it serveth, and that
feares not to tell a lie when it little importeth another man, is not sufficiently true. My mind of her
own complexion detesteth falsehood, and hateth to

think on it. I feele an inward bashfulnes and a stinging remorse if at any time it scape me, as sometimes it doth if unpremeditated occasions surprise me. A man must not alwaies say all he knowes, for that were follie : but what a man speakes ought to be agreeing to his thoughts, otherwise it is impiety. I know not what benefit they expect that ever faine, and so uncessantly dissemble : except it be not to be beleeved, even when they speake truly.

Memory

Memory is an instrument of great service, and without which, judgement wil hardly discharge his duty, wherof I have great want. What a man will propose unto me, he must doe it by peecemeales : for, to answer to a discourse that hath many heads, lieth not in my power. I cannot receive a charge, except I have my writing tables about me : and if I must remember a discourse of any consequence, be it of any length, I am driven to this vile and miserable necessitie, to learne every word I must speake by rote ; otherwise I should never do it wel or assuredly, for feare my memory should in my greatest need faile me ; which is very hard unto me, for I must have three houres to learne three verses. Moreover, in any long discourse, the libertie or authoritie to remoove the order, to change a word, uncessantly altering the matter, makes it more difficult to be confirmed in the authors memory. And the more I distrust it, the more it troubleth me. It serveth me better by chance, and I must carelessly sollicite her, for if I urge her, she is astonished ; and if it once beginne to waver, the more I sound her, the more entangled and intricate she proveth. She wil wait upon me when she list, not when I please. And what I feele in my memorie, I feele in many other parts of mine. I eschew commandement, duty, and compulsion. What I doe easily and naturally, if I resolve to doe it by expresse and prescribed appointment, I can then doe it no more. Even in my body, those parts that have some liberty, and more particular jurisdiction, doe sometimes refuse to obey me if at any time I appoint and enjoine them to doe me some necessarie services. . . A man whose thoughts are busie about other matters, shall very neere within an inch keepe and alwaies hit one selfe same number and measure of paces, in a place where he walketh ; but if heedily he endevour to measure and count them, he shall finde that what he did by nature and chance, he cannot doe it so exactly by desseign.

My library (which, for a countrey library, may passe for a very faire one) is seated in a corner of my house : if any thing come into my minde, that either I must goe seeke or write in it, for feare I should forget it in crossing of my court, I must desire some other body to remember the same for me. If speaking, I embolden my selfe never so little to digresse from my discourse, I do ever lose it ; which makes me to keepe my selfe in my speech, forced, neere and close. Those that serve me, I must ever call them either by their office or countrey : for I finde it very hard to remember names. Well may I say it hath three syllables, that its sound is harsh, or that it beginneth or endeth with such a letter. And should I live long, I doubt not but I might forget mine own name, as some others have done heretofore.

His ignorance

There is no spirit so wretched or so brutish, wherein some particular facultie is not seene to shine ; and none so low buried, but at one hole or other it will sally out sometimes. And how it commeth to passe that a minde blinde and slumbering in all other things, is in some particular effects, lively, cleare, and excellent, a man must inquire of cunning masters. But those are the faire spirits which are universall, open, and readie to all, if not instructed, at least to be instructed. Which I alleage to accuse mine : for, be it either through weakenesse, or retchlessenesse (and to be carelesse of that which lieth at our feet, which wee have in our hands, which neerest concerneth the use of life, is a thing farre from my dogma or doctrine) there is none so simple or so ignorant as mine, in divers such common matters, and of which, without imputation or shame, a man should never be ignorant ; whereof I must needs tell some examples. I was borne and brought up in the countrie, and amidst husbandry : I have since my predecessours quit me the place and possession of the goods I enjoy, both businesse and husbandry in hand, I cannot yet cast account either with penne or counters. There are divers of our French coines I know not : nor can I distinguish of one graine from another, be it in the field or in the barne, unlesse it be very apparent : nor do I scarcely know the difference betweene the cabige or lettice in my garden. I understand not the names of the most usuall tooles about husbandrie, nor of the meanest principles of tillage, which most children know. I was never skilfull in mechanicall arts, nor in traffike or knowledge of merchandize, nor in the diversitie and nature of fruits, wines, or cates, nor can I make a hawke, physike a horse, or teach a dogge.   And since I must make ful shew of my shame or ignorance, it is not yet a moneth since that I was found to be ignorant wherto leven served to make bread withall. . .

Bk. II, ch. 17, *Of Presumption*

Health

Health is a very precious jewell, and the onely thing that in pursuite of it deserveth a man should not onely employ time, labour, sweate and goods, but also life to get it ; forasmuch as without it life becommeth injurious unto us.   Voluptuousnes, science and vertue, without it, tarnish and vanish away. . . Surely my heart is not so pufft up, nor so windy, that a solide, fleshy and marrowy pleasure as health is, I should change it for an imaginary spirituall and airy delight.   Renowne or glory (were it that of Aymons foure sons) is over deerely bought by a man of my humour, if it cost him but three violent fits of the chollike.   Give me health a Gods name.

Bk. II, ch. 37, *Of the Resemblance between Children
and Fathers*

Man a mixture of qualities

Our composition, both publike and private, is full of imperfection ; yet is there nothing in nature unserviceable, no not inutility it selfe ; nothing thereof hath beene insinuated in this huge universe but holdeth some fit place therein. Our essence is cymented with evil qualities ; ambition, jealosie, envy, revenge, superstition, dispaire, lodge in us, with so naturall a possession, as their image is also discerned in beasts : yea and cruelty, so unnaturall a vice : for in the middest of compassion, we inwardly feele a kinde of bitter-sweet-pricking of malicious delight to see others suffer ; and children feele it also.

The seed of which qualities, who should roote out of man, should ruine the fundamental conditions of our life : In matter of policy likewise some necessary functions are not onely base, but faulty : vices finde therein a seate and employ themselves in the stitching up of our frame ; as poysons in the preservations of our health. If they become excusable because wee have neede of them, and that common necessity effaceth their true property, let us resigne the acting of this part to hardy Citizens, who sticke not to sacrifice their honours and consciences, as those of old, their lives, for their Countries availe and safety. We that are more weake had best assume taskes of more ease and lesse hazard. The Commonwealth requireth some to betray, some to lie, and some to massaker : leave we that commission to people more obedient and more pliable.

Bk. III, ch. 1, *Of Profit and Honesty*

Of Repenting

Others fashion man, I repeat him ; and represent a particular one, but ill made ; and whom were I to forme a new, he should be far other than he is ; but he is now made. And though the lines of my picture change and vary, yet loose they not themselves. The world runnes all on wheeles. All things therein moove without intermission; yea, the earth, the rockes of Caucasus, and the Pyramides of Aegypt, both with the publike and their own motion. Constancy it selfe is nothing but a languishing and wavering dance. I cannot settle my object; it goeth so unquietly and staggering, with a naturall drunkennesse; I take it in this plight, as it is at the instant I ammuse my selfe about it, I describe not th' essence but the passage; not a passage from age to age, or as the people reckon, from seaven yeares to seaven, but from day to day, from minute to minute. My history must be fitted to the present. I may soone change, not onely fortune, but intention. It is a counter-roule of divers and variable accidents or irresolute imaginations, and sometimes contrary; whether it be that my selfe am other, or that I apprehend subjects by other circumstances and considerations. Howsoever, I may perhaps gaine-say my selfe, but truth (as Demades said) I never gaine-say. Were my mind setled, I would not essay, but resolve my selfe. It is still a Prentise and a probationer.

I propose a meane life and without luster; 'Tis all one. All morall Philosophy can be fastened as well to a popular and private life as to one of richer stuffe. Every man beareth the whole stampe of humane condition.

Vice leaveth, as an ulcer in the flesh, a repentance in the soule, which still scratcheth and bloodieth it selfe. For reason effaceth other griefes and sorrowes, but engendereth those of repentance: the

more yrkesome because inward : as the colde and
heate of agues is more offensive then that which
comes outward. . .

In like manner there is no goodnesse but gladdeth
an honest disposition. There is truely I wot not
what kinde or congratulation of well doing which
rejoyceth in ourselves, and a generous pride that
accompanieth a good conscience. A minde couragiously vicious may happily furnish it selfe with
security, but shee cannot be fraught with this selfe-
joyning delight and satisfaction.   It is no smal pleasure for one to feele himselfe preserved from the
contagion of an age so infected as ours, and to say
to himselfe ; could a man enter and see even into
my soule, yet shold he not finde me guilty either
of the affliction or ruine of any body, nor culpable
of envie or revenge, nor of publike offence against
the lawes, nor tainted with innovation, trouble or
sedition ; nor spotted with falsifying of my word :
and although the libertie of times alowed and taught
it every man, yet could I never be induced to touch
the goods or dive into the purse of any French man,
and have alwayes lived upon mine own as wel in
time of war as peace : nor did I ever make use of any
poore mans labor without reward. . .

One may disavow and disclaime vices that surprise us, and whereto our passions transport us ; but
those which by long habite are rooted in a strong
and ankred in a powerfull will, are not subject to
contradiction.   Repentance is but a denying of our
will, and an opposition of our fantasies which diverts
us here and there. It makes some disavow their
former vertue and continencie. . .

These originall qualities are not grubd out, they

are but covered and hidden.   The Latine tongue is
to me in a manner naturall ; I understand it better
then French : but it is now fortie yeares I have not
made use of it to speake, nor much to write ; yet in
some extreame emotions and suddaine passions,
wherein I have twice or thrice falne, since my yeares
of discretion, and namely, once, when my father
being in perfect health, fell all along upon me in a
swoune, I have ever, even from my very hart uttered
my first words in latine : nature rushing and by
force expressing it selfe, against so long a custome. . .

Looke a little into the course of our experience.
There is no man (if he listen to himselfe) that doth
not discover in himselfe a peculiar forme of his, a
swaying forme, which wrestleth against art and
education, and against the tempests of passions,
which are contrary unto it.

But those other sinnes, so often reassumed, determined and advised upon, whether they be of
complexion, or of profession and calling, I cannot
conceive how they should so long be settled in one
same courage, unlesse the reason and conscience
of the sinner were thereunto inwardly privie and
constantly willing.   And how to imagine or fashion
the repentance thereof, which, he vanteth, doth
some times visit him, seemeth somewhat hard unto
me. . .

I find no humour so easie to be counterfeited as
Devotion, if one conforme not his life and conditions
to it.   Its essence is abstruse and concealed, its ap-
parances easy and ostentatious.

For my part, I may in generall wish to be other
then I am ; I may condemne and mislike my uni-

versall forme, I may beseech God to grant me an undefiled reformation, and excuse my naturall weakenesse : but meeseemeth I ought not to tearme this
repentance, no more then the displeasure of being
neither Angell nor Cato. . .

When I consult with my age of my youthes pro-
ceedings, I finde that commonly (according to my
opinion), I managed them in order. This is all my
resistance is able to performe. I flatter not my
selfe : in like circumstances, I should ever be the
same. It is not a spot, but a whole dye that staynes
mee. I acknowledge no repentance, that is super-
ficiall, meane, and ceremonious. It must touch me
on all sides before I can terme it repentance. It
must pinch my entrailes, and afflict them as deepely
and throughly as God himselfe beholds mee.

Moreover, I hate that accidentall repentance
which olde age brings with it.

Hee that in ancient times said he was beholden
to yeares because they had ridde him of voluptuousnesse, was not of mine opinion. I shall never give
impuissance thankes for any good it can do me :
. . . Our appetites are rare in olde-age : the blowe
overpassed, a deepe saciety seazeth upon us : Therein
I see no conscience. Fretting care and weakenesse
imprint in us an effeminate and drowzie vertue. . .

Youth and pleasure have not heretofore prevailed
so much over me, but I could ever (even in the midst
of sensualities) discerne the face of sinne : nor can
the distaste which yeares bring on me, at this instant, keepe mee from discerning that of voluptuousnesse in vice. Now I am no longer in it, I judge of
it as if I were still there. I who lively and attentively
examine my reason, finde it to be the same that

possessed me in my most dissolute and licentious age. . .

Should one present that former concupiscence unto it, I feare it would be of lesse power to sustaine it than heretofore it hath beene. I see in it, by it selfe no increase of judgement, nor accesse of bright-nesse ; what it now judgeth, it did then. Where-fore if there be any amendment, 'tis but diseased. . .

I approached the nearest I could unto amendment and regularity, when I should have enjoyed the same ; I should be ashamed and vexed that the misery and mishap of my old age could exceede the health, attention, and vigor of my youth : and that I should be esteemed, not for what I have beene, but for what I have ceased to be. . .

I therefore renounce these casuall and dolourous reformations. God must touch our heartes ; our conscience must amende of it selfe, and by re-in-forcement of our reason, not by the enfeebling of our strength. Voluptuousnesse in it selfe is neither pale nor discoloured to bee discerned by bleare and troubled eyes. Wee should affect temperance and chastity for it selfe, and for Gods cause, who hath ordained them unto us : that which catarrhs bestow upon us, and which I am beholden to my chollicke, is neither temperance nor chastitie. A man cannot boast of contemning or combating sensuality if hee see her not, or know not her grace, her force, and most attractive beauties. I know them both, and therefore may speake it. But mee thinks our soules in age are subject unto more importunate diseases and imperfections then they are in youth. I said so, being young, when my beardlesse chinne was upbraided me ; and I say it againe now that my gray

beard gives me authority. We entitle wisdome, the
frowardnesse of our humours, and the distaste of
present things ; but in truth wee abandon not vices
so much as we change them ; and in mine opinion
for the worse. Besides a sillie and ruinous pride,
combersome tattle, wayward and unsotiable humours, superstition, and a ridiculous carking for
wealth, when the use of it is well-nigh lost, I finde
the more envie, injustice, and malignity in it. It
sets more wrinckles in our minds then on our fore-
heads : nor are there any spirits, or very rare ones,
which in growing old taste not sowrely and mus-
tily. . .

Old Age

What Metamorphoses have I seene it daily make
in divers of mine acquaintances ? It is a powerfull
maladie which naturally and imperceptibly glideth
into us : There is required great provision of study,
heed, and precaution to avoid the imperfections
wherewith it chargeth us ; or at least to weaken their
further progresse. I finde that notwithstanding all
my entrenchings, by little and little it getteth ground
upon me : I hold out as long as I can, but know not
whither at length it will bring me. Happe what
happe will, I am pleased the world know from what
height I tumbled.

Bk. III, ch. 2, Of Repenting

Three Commerces

Friends. The end or scope of this commerce is
principally and simply familiarity, conference and
frequentation : the exercise of mindes, without other

fruite. In our discourses all subjects are alike to
me : I care not though they want either waight or
depth ; grace and pertinency are never wanting ; all
therein is tainted with a ripe and constant judgement,
and commixt with goodnesse, liberty, cheereful-
nesse, and kindnesse. It is not onely in the subject
of Laws and affaires of Princes, that our spirit sheweth it's beautie, grace and vigor : It sheweth them as
much in private conferences. I know my people
by their very silence and smyling, and peradventure
discover them better at a Table then sitting in serious
counsell. . .

Women. The company of faire and society of
honest women is likewise a sweet commerce for
me. . .

It is folly to fasten all ones thoughts upon it, and
with a furious and indiscret affection to engage himselfe unto it : But on the otherside, to meddle with
it without love or bond of affection, as Comedians
do, to play a common part of age and manners, without ought of their owne but bare-conned words,
is verily a provision for ones safety : and yet but a
cowardly one. . .

Books. In effect I make no other use of them
then those who know them not. I enjoy them, as
a miser doth his gold ; to know that I may enjoy
them when I list, my mind is setled and satisfied
with the right of possession. I never travel without bookes, nor in peace nor in warre : yet doe I
passe many dayes and moneths without using them.
It shall be anon, say I, or to-morrow, or when I
please ; in the meane while the time runnes away,
and passeth without hurting me. For it is wonder-

full what repose I take, and how I continue in this consideration, that they are at my elbow to delight me when time shall serve ; and in acknowledging what assistance they give unto my life. This is the best munition I have found in this humane peregrination, and I extremely bewaile those men of understanding that want the same. I accept with better will all other kindes of ammusements, how slight soever, forsomuch as this cannot faile me. At home I betake me somewhat the oftner to my library, whence all at once I command and survey all my houshold.

It is seated in the chiefe entrie of my house, thence I behold under me my garden, my base court, my yard, and looke even into most roomes of my house. There without order, without method, and by peece-meales I turne over and ransacke, now one booke and now another. Sometimes I muse and rave ; and walking up and downe I endight and en-register these my humours, these my conceits. It is placed on the third storie of a tower. The lowermost is my Chapell ; the second a chamber with other lodgings, where I often lie, because I would be alone. Above it is a great ward-robe. It was in times past the most unprofitable place of all my house. There I pass the greatest part of my lives dayes, and weare out most houres of the day. I am never there a nights. Next unto it is a handsome neat cabinet, able and large enough to receive fire in winter, and very pleasantly windowen. And if I feared not care more than cost (care which drives and diverts me from all businesse), I might easily joyne a convenient gallerie of a hundred paces long

and twelve broad on each side of it, and upon one
floore ; having already, for some other purpose,
found all the walles raised unto a convenient height.
Each retired place requireth a walke.   My thoughts
are prone to sleepe if I sit long.   My minde goes not
alone, as if legs did moove it.   Those that studie
without bookes are all in the same case.   The forme
of it is round, and hath no flat side, but what serveth
for my table and chaire : In which bending or cir-
cling manner, at one looke it offereth me the full sight
of all my books, set round about upon shelves or
desks, five rancks one upon another.   It hath three
bay-windowes, of a farre-extending, rich and un-
resisted prospect, and is in diameter sixteene paces
void.   In winter I am lesse continually there : for
my house (as the name of it importeth) is pearched
upon an overpearing hillocke ; and hath no part
more subject to all wethers then this : which pleaseth
me the more, both because the accesse unto it is
somwhat troublesome and remote, and for the
benefit of the exercise which is to be respected ; and
that I may the better seclude my selfe from companie, and keepe incrochers from me : There is my
seat, that is my throne.   I endevour to make my
rule therein absolute, and to sequester that only
corner from the communitie of wife, of children
and of acquaintance.   Else-where I have but a
verball authoritie, of confused essence.   Miserable
in my minde is he who in his owne home hath no
where to be to himselfe ; where hee may particularly
court, and at his pleasure hide or with-draw selfe.

          Bk. III, ch. 3, *Of Three Commerces or Societies*

Diversion

I was once neerely touched with a heavy displeasure, according to my complexion, and yet more just then heavie : I had peradventure lost my selfe in it, had I only relied upon mine owne strength. Needing a vehement diversion to with-draw me from it, I did by Arte and studie make my selfe a Lover, whereto my age assisted me ; love relieved and diverted me from the pain which friendship had caused me. So is it in all things else. A bitter imagination holdeth me ; I finde it a shorter course to alter and divert, then to tame and vanquish the same : if I cannot substitute a contrary unto it, at least I present another unto it. Change ever easeth, varietie dissolveth, and shifting dissipateth. If I cannot buckle with it, I flie from it : and in shunning it, I stray and double from it. Shifting of place, occupation and company, I save my selfe amid the throng of other studies and ammusements, where it loseth my tracke, and so I slip away.

Bk. III, ch. 4, *Of Diverting and Diversions*

Excess of severity in age

The conditions of age do but over-much admonish, instruct, and preach unto me. From the excesse of jollity, I am falne into the extreame of severity : more peevish and more untoward. Therefore, I do now of purpose somewhat give way unto licentious allurements ; and now and then employ my minde in wanton and youthfull conceits, wherein she recreates hir selfe. I am now but too much setled ; too heavy and too ripe. My yeares read me daily a lesson of coldnesse and temperance. My body shunneth disorder and feares it : it hath his turne to direct the minde toward reformation ; his turne also to rule and sway ; and that more rudely and imperiously. Be I awake or a sleepe, it doth not permit me one houre but to ruminate on instruction, on death, on patience, and on repentance. As I have heretofore defended my selfe from pleasure, so I now ward my selfe from temperance : it haleth me too far back, and even to stupidity. I will now every way be master of my selfe. Wisdome hath hir excesses, and no lesse need of moderation then follie. . .

Health

Our schollers are to blame, who searching the causes of our mindes extraordinary fits and motions, besides they ascribe some to a divine fury, to love, to warre-like fiercenesse, to Poesie, and to Wine, if they have not also allotted health her share : a health, youthfull, lusty, vigorous, full, idle, such as heretofore the Aprill of my yeares and security offered me by fittes. That fire of jocondnesse stirreth up lively and bright sparkles in our mind beyond our naturall brightnesse and amongst the most working, if not the most passionate Enthusiasmes or inspirations. . .

Hatred of austerity

I love a lightsome and civill discretion, and loathe a roughnes and austerity of behaviour : suspecting every peevish and way ward countenance. . .

Vertue is a pleasant and buxom quality. Few I

know will snarle at the liberty of my writings, that
have not more cause to snarle at their thoughts-
loosenes. . .

I hate a way ward and sad disposition, that glided
over the pleasures of his life, and fastens and feedes
on miseries. As flyes that cannot cleave to smooth
and sleeke bodies, but seaze and holde on rugged
and uneven places; or as Cupping glasses, that
affect and suck none but the worst bloud. For my
part I am resolved to dare speake whatsoever I dare
do : And am displeased with thoughts not to be
published. The worst of my actions or condicions
seeme not so ugly unto me as I finde it both ugly
and base not to dare to avouch them. . .

Frankness

I greedily long to make my selfe knowne, nor
care I at what rate, so it be truly ; or, to say better,
I hunger for nothing ; but I hate mortally to be mistaken by such as shall happen to know my name. . .

Why was the acte of generation made so naturall,
so necessary and so just, seeing we feare to speake
of it without shame, and exclude it from our serious
and regular discourses ; we prononce boldly to rob,
to murther, to betray ; and this we dare not but betweene our teeth. Are we to gather by it, that the
lesse we breath out in words the more we are allowed to furnish our thoughts with ? For words
least used, least writen, and least concealed should
best be understood, and most generally knowne.
No age, no condition are more ignorant of it then
of their bread. They are imprinted in each one,
without expressing, without voice or figure. And

the sexe that doth it most, is most bound to suppresse it. It is an action we have put in the precincts of silence, whence to draw it were an offence : not to accuse or judge it. Nor dare we beare it but in circumlocution and picture.

Marriage

I see no mariages faile sooner or more troubled then such as are concluded for beauties sake, and hudled up for amorous desires. There are required more solide foundations and more constant grounds, and a more warie marching to it : this earnest youthly heate serveth to no purpose. . . A good marriage (if any there be) refuseth the company and conditions of love ; it endevoureth to present those of amity. It is a sweete society of life, full of constancy, of trust, and an infinite number of profitable and solid offices, and mutuall obligations : No woman that throughly and impartially tasteth the same, would foregoe her estate to be her husbands mistress. Be she lodged in his affection as a wife, she is much more honourably and surely lodged.

Style

Their speech is altogether full and massie, with a naturall and constant vigor : they are all epigram, not only taile, but head, stomacke, and feet. There is nothing forced, nothing wrested, nothing limping ; all marcheth with like tenour. The whole composition or text is manly, they are not bebusied about Rhetorike flowers. This is not a soft quaint eloquence, and only without offence ; it is sinnowie,

materiall, and solid ; not so much delighting, as filling and ravishing, and ravisheth most the strongest
wits. When I behold these gallant formes of expressing, so lively, so nimble, so deepe, I say not this
is to speake well, but to think well. . .

The managing and emploiment of good wits en-
deareth and giveth grace unto a tongue : not so
much innovating as filling the same with more forcible and divers services, wresting, straining and making it pliable. They bring no words unto it, but
enrich their owne, waigh-downe and cramme-in
their signification and use ; teaching it unwonted
motions ; but wisely and ingeniously. Which skill
how little it is given to all, may plainly bee discerned
by most of our moderne French Writers. They
are over-bold and scornefull, to shunne the common
trodden path : but want of invention and lacke of
discretion looseth them. There is nothing to be
seene in them but a miserable strained affectation
of strange Inke-pot termes ; harsh, cold and absurd
disguisements, which in stead of raising, pull downe
the matter. So they may gallantize and flush it in
noveltie, they care not for efficacie. To take hold
of a new farre-fetcht word, they neglect the usuall,
which often are more significant, forcible and sinnowie. I finde sufficient store of stuffe in our language, but some defect of fashion. For there is
nothing but could be framed of our Hunters gib-
brish words or strange phrases, and of our Warriours
peculiar tearmes ; a fruitfull and rich soile to borrow of. And as hearbes and trees are bettered and
fortified by being transplanted, so formes of speach
are embellished and graced by variation.

When I write I can well omit the company, and

spare the remembrance of books ; for feare they interrupt my forme. And in truth good Authours deject me too-too much, and quaile my courage. I willingly imitate that Painter who, having bunglerlike drawn and fondly represented some Cockes, forbad his boies to suffer any live Cocke to come into his shop.

For this my dissignement, it much fitteth my purpose that I write in mine owne house, in a wild country, where no man helpeth or releeveth me ; where I converse with no body that understands the Latine of his Pater noster, and as little of French. I should no doubt have done it better else where, but then the worke had beene lesse mine, whose principall drift and perfection is to be exactly mine. I could mend an accidentall errour, whereof I abound in mine unwary course ; but it were a kinde of treason to remove the imperfections from me, which in me are ordinary and constant.

Love in old age

For, as they say, 'tis good reason, that the body follow not his appetites to the mindes prejudice or dammage. But why is it not likewise reason that the minde should not follow hers to the bodies danger and hurt ? I have no other passion that keeps mee in breath. What avarice, ambition, quarels, sutes in law, or other contentions worke and effect in others who as my selfe have no assigned vacation or certaine leisure, love would performe more commodiously : it would restore me the vigilancy, sobriety, grace and care of my person ; and assure my countenance against the wrinckled frowns of age (those deformèd and wretched frownes) which else would blemish and deface the same; it would reduce me to serious, to sound and wise studies, whereby I might procure more love, and purchase more estimation: it would purge my minde from despaire of it selfe, and of its use, acquainting the same againe with it selfe: It would divert me from thousands of irksome tedious thoughts, and melancholy carking cares, wherewith the doting idlenesse and crazed condition of our age doth charge and comber us: It would restore and heat, though but in a dreame, the blood which nature forsaketh: It would uphold the drooping chinne, and somewhat strengthen or lengthen the shrunken sinewes, decaied vigour, and dulled lives-blithenesse of silly wretched man, who gallops apace to his ruine.

Bk. III, ch. 5, Upon some Verses of Virgil

Conquest of Mexico and Peru

Our world hath of late discovered another (and who can warrant us whether it be the last of his brethren, since both the Demons, the Sibylles, and all we have hitherto been ignorant of this?) no lesse-large, fully-peopled, all-things-yeelding, and mighty in strength than ours; neverthelesse so new and infantine, that it is yet to learne its A B C. It is not yet full fifty yeeres that it knew neither letters, nor waight, nor measures, nor apparell, nor corne, nor vines; But was all naked, simply-pure, in Natures lappe, and lived but with such meanes and food as its mother-nurce affoorded it. . . It was an unpolluted, harmelesse, infant world; yet have we not whipped and submitted the same unto our discipline, or schooled it by the advantage of our valour or naturall forces ; nor have wee instructed it by our justice and integrity, nor subdued by our magnanimity. Most of their answers, and a number of the negotiations we have had with them, witnesse that they were nothing short of us, not beholding to us for any excellency of naturall wit or perspicuitie or pertinency. The wonderfull, or as I may call it, amazement-breeding magnificence of the cities of Cusco and Mexico, and amongst infinite such like things, the admirable Garden of that King, where all the Trees, the fruits, the Hearbes and Plants, according to the order and greatnesse they have in a Garden, were most artificially formed in gold ; as also in his Cabinet, all the living creatures that his Countrey or his Seas produced, were cast in gold ; and the exquisite beauty of their workes, in precious Stones, in Feathers, in Cotton and in Painting, shew that they yeelded as little unto us in cunning and industrie. But concerning devotion, observance of lawes, magnanimity, integrity, liberality, loyalty and frankness, it hath greatly availed us that we had not so much as they : By which advantage they have lost, castaway, sold, undone and betraied themselves.

Touching hardinesse and courage, and as for matchlesse constancie, unmooved assurednesse, and undismaied resolution against paine, hunger and death it selfe, I will not feare to oppose the examples which I may easily finde amongst them, to the most famous ancient examples we may with all our industrie discover in all the Annales and memories of our knowen old World. For as for those

which have subdued them, let them lay aside the
wiles, the policies and stratagems which they have
emploied to cozen, to cunny-catch, and to circumvent them ; and the just astonishment which those
nations might conceive, by seeing so unexpected an
arrivall of bearded men, divers in language, in
habite, in religion, in behaviour, in forme, in countenance, and from a part of the world so distant,
and where they never heard any habitation was :
mounted upon great and unknowen monsters,
against those who had had never so much as seene
any horse, and lesse any beast whatsoever apt to
beare, or taught to carry either man or burden ;
covered with a shining and harde skinne, and armed
with slicing-keene weapons and glittering armour :
against them, who for the wonder of the glistring
of a looking-glasse or of a plaine knife would have
changed or given inestimable riches in Gold, Precious Stones and Pearles ; and who had neither the
skill nor the matter wherewith at any leasure they
could have pierced our steele : to which you may
adde the flashing-fire and thundring roare of shotte
and Harguebuses ; able to quell and daunt even
Caesar himselfe, had he beene so sodainely surprised
and as little experienced as they were ; and thus
to come unto and assault naked people, saving
where the invention of weaving of Cotton cloath
was knowne and used ; for the most altogether
unarmed, except some bowes, stones, staves and
woodden bucklers ; unsuspecting poore people, surprised under colour of amity and well-meaning
faith, overtaken by the curiosity to see strange and
unknowne things : I say, take this disparity from
the conquerors, and you deprive them of all the

occasions and cause of so many victories. When
I consider that sterne-untamed obstinacy and undanted vehemence wherewith so many thousands
of men, of women and children, do so infinite times
present themselves unto inevitable dangers, for the
defence of their Gods and liberty : This generous
obstinacy to endure all extremities, all difficulties
and death, more easily and willingly, then basely to
yeelde unto their domination, of whom they have
so abhominably beene abused : some of them choosing rather to starve with hunger and fasting, being
taken, then to accept food at their enemies handes,
so basely victorious : I perceive, that whosoever
had undertaken them man to man, without odds
of armes, of experience or of number, should have
had as dangerous a warre, or perhaps more, as any
we see amongst us.

Why did not so glorious a conquest happen under Alexander, or during the time of the ancient
Greekes and Romanes ? or why befell not so great
a change and alteration of Empires and people under such hands as would gently have polished, re-
formed and incivilized what in them they deemed
to be barbarous and rude : or would have nour-
ished and fostered those good seedes which nature
had there brought foorth : adding not onely to the
manuring of their grounds and ornaments of their
cities such artes as we had, and that no further
then had beene necessary for them, but there-withall
joyning unto the originall vertues of the country
those of the ancient Grecians and Romanes ? What
reputation and what reformation would all that
farre spredding world have found, if the examples,
demeanors and pollicies wherewith we first pre-

sented them had called and allured those uncorrupted nations to the admiration and imitation of vertue, and had established betweene them and us a brotherly society and mutuall correspondency ? How easie a matter had it beene profitably to reforme and christianly to instruct minds yet so pure and new, so willing to bee taught, being for the most part endowed with so docile, so apt and so yeelding naturall beginnings ? Whereas, contrarywise, we have made use of their ignorance and inexperience, to drawe them more easily unto treason, fraude, luxurie, avarice and all manner of inhumanity and cruelty, by the example of our life and patterne of our customes. Who ever raised the service of marchandize and benefit of traffick to so high a rate ? So many goodly citties ransacked and razed ; so many nations destroyed and made desolate ; so infinite millions of harmelesse people of all sexes, states and ages, massacred, ravaged and put to the sword ; and the richest, the fairest and the best part of the world topsiturvied, ruined and defaced for the traffick of Pearles and Pepper. Oh mechanicall victories, oh base conquest. Never did ambition, never did publik enmities, so passionately incense men against men, unto so horrible hostilities, and miserable calamities.

Certaine Spaniardes, coasting alongst the Sea in search of mines, fortuned to land in a very fertile, pleasant and well peopled country, unto the inhabitants whereof they declared their intent and shewed their accustomed perswasions ; saying, That they were quiet and well-meaning men, comming from farre-countries, being sent from the King of Castile, the greatest King of the habitable earth, unto whom the Pope, representing God on earth, had given the principality of all the Indies. That if they would become tributaries to him, they should bee most kindly used and courteously entreated. They required of them victualles for their nourishment, and some gold for the behoofe of certaine Physicall experiments. Moreover, they declared unto them the beleeving in one onely God and the trueth of our religion, which they perswaded them to embrace, adding thereto some minatorie threates. Whose answer was this : That happily they might be quiet and well meaning, but their countenance shewed them to be otherwise : As concerning their King, since he seemed to beg, he shewed to be poore and needy ; And for the Pope, who had made that distribution, he expressed himselfe a man loving dis-sention, in going about to give unto a third man a thing which was not his owne, so to make it ques-tionable and litigious amongst the ancient possessors of it. As for victualles, they should have part of their store ; And for gold, they had but little, and that it was a thing they made very small accoumpt of, as meerely unprofitable for the service of their life ; whereas all their care was but how to passe it happily and pleasantly, and therefore, what quan-tity soever they should finde, that onely excepted which was employed about the service of their Gods, they might bouldly take it. As touching one onely God, the discourse of him had very well pleased them ; but they would by no meanes change their religion under which they had for so long time lived so happily ; and that they were not ac-customed to take any counsell, but of their friends and acquaintance. As concerning their menaces, it was a signe of want of judgement to threaten those whose nature, condition, power and meanes was to them unknowne. And therefore they should with all speed hasten to quit their dominions (forsomuch as they were not wont remonstrances of armed people, namely, of strangers) otherwise they would deale with them as they had done with such others, shewing them the heads of certaine men sticking upon stakes about their Citie, which had lately beene executed. Loe here an example of the stammering of this infancy. . .

Of two the most mighty and glorious Monarkes of that world, and peradventure of all our Westerne parts, Kings over so many Kings, the last they deposed and overcame; He of Peru, having by them been taken in a battell, and set at so excessive a ransome that it exceedeth all beliefe, and that truely paide: and by his conversation having given them apparant signes of a free, liberall, undanted, and constant courage, and declared to be of a pure, noble, and well composed understanding; a humour possessed the conquerors, after they had most insolently exacted from him a Million three hundred five and twenty thousand, and five hundred waights of golde, besides the silver and other precious things, which amounted to no lesse a summe (so that their horses were all shood of massive gold), to discover (what disloyalty or treachery soever it might cost them) what the remainder of this Kings treasure might be, and without controlment enjoy whatever he might have hidden or concealed from them. Which to compasse, they forged a false accusation

and proofe against him, that hee practised to raise
his provinces, and intended to induce his subjects
to some insurrection, so to procure his liberty.
Whereupon, by the very judgement of those who
had complotted this forgery and treason against
him, hee was condemned to be publikely hanged
and strangled ; having first made him to redeeme
the torment of being burned alive by the baptisme
which at the instant of his execution in charity they
bestowed upon him ; a horrible and the like never
heard of accident, which neverthelesse he undis-
maiedly endured with an unmoved manner and
truly-royall gravity, without ever contradicting
himselfe either in countenance or speech. And
then, somewhat to mitigate and circumvent those
silly unsuspecting people, amazed and astonished
at so strange a spectacle, they counterfeited a great
mourning and lamentation for his death, and appointed his funeralls to bee solemnely and sump-
tuously celebrated.

Bk. III, ch. 6, Of Coaches

On Conversation

The most fruitfull and naturall exercise of our
spirit is, in my selfe-pleasing conceit, conference.
The use whereof I finde to be more delightsome
then any other action of our life. . .

When I am impugned or contraried, then is mine
attention and not mine anger stirred up : I advance
my selfe toward him that doth gainesay and instruct
me. The cause of truth ought to be the common
cause both to one and other. . .

I feast, I cherish and I embrace truth, where and in whom soever I finde it, and willingly and merily yeeld my selfe unto her, as soone as I see but her approach, though it be a farre-off, I lay downe my weapon and yeeld my selfe vanquished. And alwayes provided one persist not or proceede therein, with an over-imperious stiffnesse or commanding surlinesse, I am well pleased to be reprooved. And I often accommodate my selfe unto my accusers more by reason of civility then by occasion of amendment: loving by the facility of yeelding to gratifie and foster their libertie, to teach or advertise me. . .

It is impossible to treate quietly and dispute orderly with a foole. My judgement is not onely corrupted under the hand of so imperious a maister, but my conscience also. Our disputations ought to be forbidden and punished, as other verball crimes. What vice raise they not, and heape up together, being ever swayed and commanded by choller? First we enter into enmity with the reasons, and then with the men. We learne not to dispute, except it be to contradict; and every man contradicting and being contradicted, it commonly followeth that the fruit of disputing is to lose and to disanull the trueth. . .

Agitation and hunting properly belong to us; wee are not excusable to conduct the same ill and impertinently, but to misse the game and faile in taking, that's another matter. For wee are borne to quest and seeke after trueth; to possesse it belongs to a greater power. . .

Obstinacy and earnestnesse in opinion is the surest tryall of folly and selfe conceit. Is there any thing so assured, so resolute, so disdainfull, so contemplative, so serious and so grave, as the Asse ? . . .

May we not commixe with the title of conference and communication the sharpe and interrupted discourses which mirth and familiarity introduceth amongst friends, pleasantly dallying and wittily jesting one with another ? An exercise to which my naturall blithnesse makes me very apt.

Bk. III, ch. 8, *Of the Art of Conferring*

Words

When shall I come unto an end of representing a continuall agitation or uncessant alteration of my thoughts, what subject soever they happen upon, since Diomedes filled six thousand bookes only with the subject of Grammar ? What is idle babling like to produce, since the faltring and liberty of the tongue hath stuft the world with so horrible a multitude of volumes ? So many words onely for words. Oh Pythagoras, why didst not thou conjure this tempest ? . . . It is no mockerie : Scribling seemeth to be a Symthome or passion of an irregular and licentious age. When writ we ever so much as we have done since our intestine troubles, or when filled the Romans so many volumes as in the times of their ruine ?

Contrary to others, I finde my selfe more given to devotion in prosperous then adverse fortune . . . and I rather looke on heaven with a chearefull eye, to thanke it, then to implore it. I am more carefull to encrease my health when it smiles upon me, then to recover it when I have lost it.

Bk. III, ch. 9, *Of Vanitie*

Revolution

Nothing doth so neerely touch and so much over-
lay a State as innovation : Onely change doth give
forme to injustice and scope to tyranny. If some
one peece be out of square, it may be underpropt :
one may oppose himselfe against the alteration and
corruption naturall to all things so that it draw us
not too far from our beginnings and grounded principles. But to undertake to re-erect and found
againe so huge a masse, and change the foundations
of so vast a frame, belongeth onely to them who,
instead of purging, deface, and in lieu of cleansing,
scrape out ; who will amend particular faults by
an universall confusion and cure diseases by death :
The world is unapt to cure it selfe : So impatient
with that which vexeth or grieveth it, that it only
aimeth to ridd it selfe of it, never regarding at what
rate.

Civil war

I have a thousand times gone to bed in mine house,
imagining I should the very same night either have
beene betrayed or slaine in my bed ; compounding
and conditioning with fortune that it might be without apprehension of feareful astonishment and lan-
guishment. . . What remedie ? It is the place where
my selfe and most of my ancestors were borne :
therein have they placed their affection and their
name. Wee harden our selves unto whatsoever
wee accustome our selves. And to a wretched condition, as ours is, custome hath beene a most favourable present, given us by nature, which enureth and

lulleth our sense asleepe to the suffring of divers
evils. Civill warres have this one thing worse then
other warres, to cause every one of us to make a
watch-tower of his owne house. . .

I sometimes draw the meanes to strengthen my
selfe against these considerations, from carelesnesse
and idlenesse, which also in some sort bring us unto
resolution. It often befalleth me, with some pleasure, to imagine what mortall dangers are, and to expect them. I do even hood-winkt, with my head
in my bosome and with stupiditie, plunge my selfe
into death, without considering or knowing it, as
into a deepe, hollow and bottomlesse abysse, which
at one leape doth swallow me up, and at an instant
doth cast me into an eternall slumber, full of in-
sipiditie and indolencie.

Paris

I can never mutinie so much against France but
I must needes looke on Paris with a favourable eye :
It hath my hart from my infancy, whereof it hath
befalne me as of excellent things : the more other
faire and stately cities I have seene since, the more
hir beauty hath power and doth still usurpingly
gaine upon my affection. I love that Citie for her
owne sake, and more in her onely subsisting and
owne being then when it is full fraught and embellished with forraine pompe : I love her so tenderly
that even hir spotts, her blemishes and hir warts are
deare unto me. I am no perfect Frenchman, but by
this great-matchlesse Citie, great in people, great in
regard of the felicitie of her situation ; but above al
great and incomparable in varietie and diversitie of

commodities : The glory of France, and one of the noblest and chiefe ornaments of the world. God of his mercy free hir, and chase away all our divisions from hir : Being entirely united to hir selfe, I finde hir defended from all other violence. I forewarne hir, that of all factions, that shall be the worst which shall breed discord and sedition in hir. And for hir sake, I onely feare hir selfe. And surely I am in as great feare for hir as for any other part of our state. So long as she shall continue, so long shall I never want a home or retreat to retire and shrowd my selfe at all times : a thing able to make me forget the regret of all other retreates.

Travel

Besides these reasons, I deem travell to be a profitable exercise. The minde hath therein a continuall excitation, to marke things unknowne, and note new objects. And as I have often said : 'I know no better schoole to fashion a man's life then uncessantly to propose unto him the diversitie of so many other mens lives, customes, humors, and fantasies ; and make him taste or apprehend one so perpetuall variety of our natures, shapes, or formes. Therein the body is neither absolutely idle nor wholly troubled, and that moderate agitation doth put him into breath.' My selfe, as crazed with the collicke as I am, can sit eight, yea sometimes ten houres on horse-backe, without wearinesse or tyring. No weather is to me so contrary as the scorching heat of the parching Sunne. . . I love rainy and durty weather as duckes doe. The change either of aire or climate doth nothing distemper mee. All heavens

are alike to me, I am never vexed or beaten, but with
internall alterations, such as I produce my selfe,
which surprise and possesse me least in times of
Wayfairing. It is a hard matter to make me resolve of any journey ; but if I be once on the way,
I hold out as long and as farre as another. I strive
as much in small as I labour in great enterprises ;
and to prepare my selfe for a short journey or to
visite a friend, as to undertake a farre set voiage.
I have learnt to frame my journeyes after the Spanish
fashion, all at once and out-right, great and reasonable. And in extreme heats I travell by night, from
Sunne-set to Sunne rising. . . My slothfulnesse to
rise in the morning alloweth such as follow mee
sufficient leasure to dine before wee take horse. As
for me, I never feed over-late : I commonly get an
appetite in eating, and no otherwise : I am never
hungry but at the table. Some complaine that being
maried, and well strucken in yeares, I have enured
my selfe, and beene pleased to continue this exercise.
They doe me wrong. The best time for a man to
leave his house is when he hath so ordered and settled the same that it may continue without him ;
and when he hath so disposed his affaires, that they
may answere the ancient course and wonted forme.
It is much more indiscretion, and an argument of
want of judgement, to goe from home and leave no
trusty guard in his house. . .

I require in a maried woman the Oeconomicall
vertue above all others. Wherein I would have her
absolutely skilfull, since by my absence I commit
the whole charge and bequeath the full government
of my houshold to her.

I see (and that to my griefe) in divers houses the

master or goodman come home at noone all weary,
durty and dusty, with drudging and toiling about
his businesse; when the mistresse or good-wife is
either scarce up, or if shee bee, she is yet in her
closet, dressing, decking, smugging, or trimming of
her selfe. It is a thing onely fitting Queenes or
Princes; whereof some doubt might be made. It
is ridiculous and unjust that the ostentation and idlenesse of our wives should be fostered with our sweat
and maintained by our labour.

Absence in marriage and friendship

Concerning duties of wedlocke-friendship, which
some happily imagine to be interested or prejudiced
by the husbands absence, I beleeve it not. Contrariwise, it is a kinde of intelligence that easily
growes cold by an over-continuall assistance, and
decaieth by assiduitie; for to stand still at racke
and manger breedeth a satietie. Every strange
woman seemeth to us an honest woman: And all
feele by experience that a continuall seeing one another cannot possibly represent the pleasure men
take by parting and meeting againe. These inter-
ruptions fill mee with a new kinde of affection
toward mine owne people, and yeeld me the use of
my house more pleasing: vicissitude doth now and
then en-earnest my minde toward one, and then
toward another. I am not ignorant how true amitie
hath armes long enough to embrace, to claspe and
holde from one corner of the world unto another;
namely in this, where is a continuall communication of offices that cause the obligation and revive
the remembrance thereof.

In truly-perfect friendship, wherein I presume to have some skill and well-grounded experience, I give my selfe more unto my friend than I draw him unto me. I doe not onely rather love to do him good, then he should doe any to me, but also that he should rather doe good unto himselfe then unto me : For then doth he me most good when he doth it to himselfe. And if absence be either pleasing or beneficiall unto him, it is to me much more pleasing then his presence ; and that may not properly be termed absence where meanes and waies may be found to enter-advertise one another. I have heeretofore made good use and reaped commoditie by our absence and distance. Wee better replenished the benefit and extended further the possession of life by being divided and farre-asunder : He lived, he rejoiced, and he saw for me and I for him, as fully as if he had beene present : Being together, one partie was idle : We confounded one another. The separation of the place made the conjunction of our mindes and wills the richer. This insatiate and greedy desire of corporall presence doth somewhat accuse weakenesse in the enjoyment of soules.

Age for travel

Concerning age, which some allege against me, it is cleane contrary. It is for youth to subject and bondage it selfe to common opinions, and by force to constraine it selfe for others. It may fit the turne of both the people and it selfe : We have but overmuch to doe with our selves alone. According as naturall commodities faile us, let us sustaine our selves by artificiall meanes. It is injustice to excuse youth in following her pleasures, and forbid age to devise and seeke them.

Travel in old age

"But at your age you will never returne home again from such a farre journie." What care I for that? I undertake it not either to returne or to perfect the same. I onely undertake it to be in motion: So long as the motion pleaseth me, and I walke that I may walke. Those runne not that runne after a Benefice or after a Hare: But they runne that runne at barriers and to exercise their running. My desseigne is every where divisible, it is not grounded on great hopes: each day makes an end of it. Even so is my lifes voiage directed. Yet I have seene divers farre countries where I would have beene glad to have beene staied. Why not? If Chrysippus, Diogenes, Cleanthes, Antipater, and Zeno, with so many other wise men of that roughly-severe and severely-strict Sect, forsooke their Countries (without just cause to be offended with them), onely to enjoy another aire? Truly the greatest griefe of my peregrinations is, that I cannot have a firme resolution to establish my abiding where I would.

Travel

And then it is for those who by their urgent affaires are compelled to travell in the midst of deepe Winter, and amongst the Grisons, to be surprized by such extreamities in their journies. But I, who for the most part never travell but for pleasure, will neither bee so ill advised nor so simply guided. If the way be foule on my right hand, I take the left. If I find my selfe ill at ease or unfit to ride, I stay at home. Which doing, and observing this course, in very truth I see no place and come no where that is not as pleasant, as convenient, and as commodious as mine owne house. True it is that I ever find superfluitie superfluous, and observe a kind of troublesomenesse in delicatenesse and plenty. Have I omitted or left any thing behind me that was worth the seeing? I returne backe; It is ever my way, I am never out of it. I trace no certaine line, neither straight nor crooked. Comming to any strange place, finde I not what was told mee? As it often fortuneth that others judgements agree not with mine, and have most times found them false, I grieve not at my labour; I have learned that what was reported to bee there is not.

I have my bodies complexion as free and my taste as common as any man in the world. The diversity of fashions betweene one and other Nations concerneth me nothing, but by the varieties-pleasure. Each custome hath his reason. Bee the trenchers or dishes of wood, of pewter, or of earth; bee my meate boyled, rosted, or baked; butter or oyle, and that of Olives or of Wall-nuts, hot or colde, I make no difference, all is one to me. And as one that is growing old, I accuse this generous facultie, and had need that delicatenesse and choice should stay the indiscretion of my appetite, and sometime ease and solace my stomacke. When I have beene out of France, and that to do me curtesie some have asked me Whether I would be served after the French

maner, I have jested at them, and have ever
thrust-in amongst the tables fullest of strangers. I
am ashamed to see our men besotted with this foolish humor, to fret and chafe when they see any
fashions contrary to theirs. They thinke themselves
out of their element when they are out of their
Village. Where ever they come they keepe their
owne country fashions, and hate, yea and abhorre
all strange manners. Meet they a countriman of
theirs in Hungary, they feast that good fortune.
And what doe they? Marry close and joyne together, to blame, to condemne, and to scorne so
many barbarous fashions as they see. And why not
Barbarous since not French? Nay, happily they
are the better sort of men that have noted and so
much exclaimed against them. Most take going out
but for comming home. They travell close and
covered, with a silent and incommunicable prudence, defending themselves from the contagion
of an unknowne ayre. What I speake of such puts
mee in minde in the like matter of that I have heretofore perceived in some of your young Courtiers.
They onely converse with men of their coate, and
with disdaine or pitty looke upon us as if we were
men of another world. Take away their new fan-
gled, mysterious, and affected courtly complements,
and they are out of their byase. As farre to seeke
and short of us as we of them. That saying is true;
That An honest man is a man compounded. Cleane
contrary, I travell fully glutted with our fashions:
Not to seeke Gaskoines in Sicilie, I have left over
many at home. I rather seeke for Graecians and
Persians. Those I accost, Them I consider, and

with such I endevour to be acquainted ; to that I lend and therein I employ my selfe. And which is more, me seemeth I have not met with many maners that are not worth ours. . .

It is a rare chaunce and seld-seene fortune, but of exceeding solace and inestimable worth, to have an honest man of a sound judgement, and of manners conformable to yours, to accompany or follow you with a good will. I have found great want of such a one in all my voyages. Which company a man must seeke with discretion and with great heed obtaine before he wander from home. With me no pleasure is fully delightsome without communication, and no delight absolute except imparted. I doe not so much as apprehend one rare conceipt, or conceive one excellent good thought in my minde, but me thinks I am much grieved to have produced the same alone and that I have no sympathizing companion to impart it unto. . .

Architas his opinion is sutable to mine, which was that it would be a thing unpleasing in the very heavens, to walke within those immense and divine and cœlestiall bodies, without the assistance of a friend or companion : Yet is it better to be alone than in tedious and foolish company. . .

I should chuse to weare out my life with my bum in the saddle, ever riding.

"Have you not more easie pastimes ? What is it you want ? Is not your house well seated, and in a good and wholesome ayre ? Sufficiently furnished and more then sufficiently capable ? . . .

"Where doe you imagine you may bee without empeachment or disturbance ? You see then there is none but you that trouble and busie your selfe :

and every where you shall follow your self, and in all places you shall complaine. For here below there is no satisfaction or content, except for brutall or divine mindes."

Wel I wot that being taken according to the bare letter, the pleasure of travell brings a testimony of unquietnesse and irresolution. Which, to say truth, are our mistrisse and predominant qualities. Yea, I confesse it : I see nothing, but in dreames or wishes whereon I may take hold. Onely varietie and the possession of diversitie doth satisfie me, if at least any thing satisfie mee.

Obedience to laws

One may bewaile the better times, but not avoide the present ; one may desire other magistrates, but notwithstanding he must obey those he hath ; And happily it is more commendable to obey the wicked than the good. So long as the image of the received, allowed, and ancient lawes of this Monarchie shall be extant and shine in any corner thereof, there will I be, there will I abide. And if by any disaster they shall chaunce to have contradiction or empeachment amongst themselves, and produce two factions, or doubtfull or hard choise ; my election shall be to avoide, and, if I can, escape this storme. In the meane while, either nature or the hazard of warre shall lend me that helping hand. I should freely have declared my selfe betweene Caesar and Pompey. But betweene those three theeves which came after, either one must have hid himselfe or followed the winde : which I deeme lawfull, when reason swayeth no longer.

Seeming carelessness of his Essays

This mingle-mangle is somewhat beside my text. I stragle out of the path ; yet it is rather by licence then by unadvisednesse : my fantasies follow one another, but sometimes a farre off, and looke one at another, but with an oblique looke. I have heretofore cast mine eyes upon some of Platoes Dialogues. . . They feare not those variances, and have a wonderfull grace in suffering themselves to bee transported by the wind, or to seeme so. The titles of my chapters embrace not allwayes the matter ; they often but glance at it by some marke. . . I love a Poeticall kinde of march, by friskes, skips, and jumps. It is an arte (saith Plato) light, nimble, fleeting, and demoniacal. There are some treatises in Plutarke where he forgets his theame, where the drift of his argument is not found but by incidencie and chaunce, all stuffed with strange matter. Marke but the vagaries in his *Daemon of Socrates*. Oh God ! what grace hath the variation, and what beautie these startings and nimble escapes ! And then most, when they seeme to employ carelesnesse and casualtie. It is the unheedie and negligent reader that loseth my subject, and not my self. Some word or other shall ever be found in a corner that hath relation to it, though closely couched.

Hatred of obscurity

And there be humors to whom understanding causeth disdaine, who because they shall not know what I meane will esteeme mee the better, and will conclude the mystery and depth of my sense by the

obscuritie, which, to speake in good earnest, I hate
as death, and would shunne it if I could avoid my
selfe.

Rome

The care and remembrance of the dead is recommended unto us. Now have I from my infancie
beene bred and brought up with these ; I have had
knowledge of the affaires of Rome, long time before
I had notice of those of my house. I knew the Cap-
itoll and its platforme, before I knew Louvre, the
pallace of our Kings in Paris ; and the River Tiber
before Seyne. I have more remembred and thought
upon the fortunes and conditions of Lucullus, Metel-
lus and Scipio, then of any of our country-men.
They are deceased, and so is my father as fully as
they ; and is as distant from me and life in eighteene
yeeres as they were in sixteene hundred ; Whose
memorie, amitie, and societie I notwithstanding omit
not to continue, to embrace and converse withall,
with a perfect and most lively union. Yea, of mine
owne inclination I am more officious toward the deceased. They can no longer helpe themselves, but
(as me seemeth) they require so much the more my
ayde ; There is Gratitude, and there appeareth she
in her perfect lustre. . .

Such as have at any time deserved friendship or
love or thanks at my hands, never lost in the same by
being no longer with me. I have better paid and
more carefully rewarded them, being absent and
when they least thought of it. I speake more
kindely and affectionately of my friends when there
is least meanes that ever it shall come to their eares.

I have heretofore undergone a hundred quarrels for the defence of Pompey and Brutus his cause. This acquaintance continueth to this day betweene us. Even of present things wee have no other holde but by our fantazie. Perceiving my selfe unfit and unprofitable for this age, I cast my selfe to that other, and am so besotted with it that the state of the said ancient, free, just and florishing Rome (for I neither love the birth nor like the old age of the same), doth interest, concerne and passionate me. And therefore can I not so often looke into the situation of their streets and houses, and those wondrous-strange ruines, that may be said to reach down to the Antipodes, but so often must I ammuse my selfe on them. Is it nature or by the error of fantasie, that the seeing of places wee know to have beene frequented or inhabited by men, whose memory is esteemed or mentioned in stories, doth in some sort move and stirre us up as much or more than the hearing of their noble deeds, or reading of their compositions ? . . . I am much delighted with the consideration of their countenance, port and abilliments. I ruminate those glorious names betweene my teeth, and make mine eares to ring with the sound of them. . . Of things but in some sort great, strange and admirable, I admire their common parts. I could wish to see them walk and suppe together, and heare their discourses. It were Ingratitude to despise and impietie to neglect the reliques or images of so many excellent, honest good men, and therewithall so valiant, which I have seene live and die ; And who by their examples, had we the wit or grace to follow them, affoord us so many notable instructions.

And Rome as it stands now deserveth to be loved,

confederated so long since and sharing titles with
our Crowne of France, the only common and universall Citie. The Soveraigne Magistrate therein
commanding is likewise acknowledged abroad. It
is the Metropolitan Citie of all Christian nations;
both French and Spaniards, and all men else, are
there at home. To be a Prince of that state, a man
needs but be of Christendome, where ever it be
seated. There's no place here on earth that the
Heavens have embraced with such influence of fa-
vors and grace, and with such constancie; even her
ruine is glorious with renowne, and swolne with
glorie.

Low-levelled as she lieth, and even in the tombe
of hir glory, she yet reserveth the lively image and
regardfull markes of Empire.

Children

Besides, I am not tied with that strong bond
which some say bindes men to future times, by the
children bearing their names, and succeeding them
in honors; And being so much to be desired, it may
be I shall wish for them so much the lesse. I am by
my selfe but overmuch tied unto the world and
fastned unto life; I am pleased to be in Fortunes
hold by the circumstances properly necessary to my
state, without enlarging her jurisdiction upon me
by other wayes; And I never thought that to be
without children were a defect, able to make mans
life lesse compleat and lesse contented. A barren
state or sterill vacation have also their peculiar commodities. Children are in the number of things that
need not greatly bee desired; especially in these

corrupted daies, wherein it would be so hard a matter to make them good.

Bk. III, ch. 9, Of Vanitie

Public duty

In regard of the common sort of men, few things touch me, or (to speake properly) sway me; for it is reason they touch, so they possesse-us not. I have great neede, both by study and discourse, to encrease this priviledge of insensibilitie, which is naturally crept farre into me. I am not wedded unto many things, and by consequence not passionate of them. I have my sight cleare, but tied to few objects; my senses delicate and gentle, but my apprehension and application hard and dull. I engage my selfe with difficulty. . .

Mine opinion is, that one should lend himselfe to others, and not give himselfe but to himselfe. Were my will easie to engage or apply it selfe, I could not last: I am over tender both by nature and custome. . . We should thriftily husband our mindes liberty, and never engage it but upon just occasions, which if we judge impartially, are very few in number. . .

It is likely that the true point of friendship, which every man oweth to himselfe, is to be found in this. Not a false amitie, which makes us embrace glory, knowledge, riches, and such like, with a principall and immoderate affection, as members of our being; nor an effeminate and indiscreet friendship, wherein hapneth as to the Ivie, which corrupts and ruines the wals it claspeth; But a sound and regular amity, equally profitable and pleasant. Who so under-

standeth all her duties and exerciseth them, hee is
rightly endenizend in the Muses cabinet ; hee hath
attained the summit of humane Wisedome and the
perfection of our happinesse. This man, knowing
exactly what hee oweth to himselfe, findeth that
he ought to employ the use of other men and of the
world unto himselfe ; which to performe, he must
contribute the duties and offices that concerne him
unto publike societie. He that lives not somewhat
to others, liveth little to himselfe.

His conduct as Mayor of Bordeaux

All publike actions are subject to uncertaine and
divers interpretations, for too many heads judge
of them. Some say of this my City-employment
(whereof I am content to speake a word, not that
it deserves it, but to make a shew of my manners in
such things) I have demeaned my selfe like one that
is too slowly mooved and with a languishing affection ; and they are not altogether void of reason. I
strive to keepe my minde and thoughts quiet . . .
from which naturall slacknesse one must not therefore inferre any proofe of disability (for, want of
care and lacke of judgement are two things) and
lesse of unkindnesse and ingratitude toward those
Citizens who to gratifie me, employed the utmost
of all the meanes they could possibly, both before
they knew me and since ; and who did much more
for me in appointing me my charge the second time,
then in choosing me the first. I love them with all
my heart, and wish them all the good that may be ;
And truly if occasion had beene offered I would
have spared nothing to have done them service. I

have stirred and laboured for them as I doe for my selfe. They are good people, warlike and generous, yet capable of obedience and discipline and fit for good employment, if they be well guided. They say likewise that I passed over this charge of mine without any deede of note or great shew. It is true. Moreover, they accuse my cessation, when almost all the world was convicted of too much doing. . .

I accuse not a Magistrate that sleepeth so they that are under him sleepe also. So sleepe the lawes. For my part I commend a gliding, an obscure and silent life. . .

He that will not thanke me for the good order and for the sweet and undisturbed rest which hath accompanied my charge, cannot at least deprive me of that part which by the title of my good fortune belongeth unto me. This is my humour, that I love as much to be happy as wise, and to attribute my successes as much to the meere grace of God as to the working of my operation. I had sufficiently published to the world my insufficiency in managing of such publike affaires : nay, there is something in me worse than insufficiency : which is, that I am not much displeased therewith, and that I endevour not greatly to cure it, considering the course of life I have determined to my selfe. Nor have I satisfied my selfe in this employment, but have almost attained what I had promised unto my selfe, and have much exceeded what I had promised those with whom I was to deal ; for I willingly promise somewhat lesse than I can performe or hope to accomplish. Of this I am assured, I have never left offence or hatred among them. To have left either

regret or desire of me, this know I at least that I
have not much wished for it.

Bk. III, ch. 10, *How one ought to govern his Will*

Rumour and Exaggeration

I have seene the birth of divers miracles in my
dayes. . . A particular errour doth first breed a
publike errour; And when his turne commeth, a
publike errour begetteth a particular errour. So
goeth all this vast frame, from hand to hand, con-
founding and composing it selfe, in such sort that
the furthest-abiding testimonie, is better instructed
of it then the nearest, and the last informed better
perswaded then the first. It is naturall progresse;
for whosoever beleeveth any thing thinkes it a deede
of charity to perswade it unto another; which that
he may the better effect, he feareth not to adde
something of his owne invention thereunto, so far
as he seeth necessary in his discourse, to supply the
resistance and defect, he imagineth to bee in anoth-
ers conception. My selfe who make an especiall
matter of conscience to lie, and care not greatly to
add credit or authority to what I say, perceive, nev-
ertheles, by the discourses I have in hand, that being
excited, either by the resistance of another or by
the heat of my naration, I swell and amplifie my
subject by my voice, motions, vigor and force of
wordes; as also by extension and amplification, not
without some prejudice to the naked truth. But
yet I doe it upon condition that to the first that
brings mee home againe, and enquireth for the bare
and simple truth at my hands, I sodainly give over

my hold, and without exaggeration, emphasis or amplification, I yeeld it unto him. A lively, earnest and ready speech as mine, is easie transported into hyperboles.

Bk. III, ch. 11, *Of the Lame or Crippel*

Socrates

Might such a man be borne now adayes, there are but few would now esteeme him. Wee discerne not graces inly or aright ; we onely perceive them by a false light set out and puft up with arte ; Such as passe under their naturall purity and simplicity doe easily escape so weake and dimme a sight as ours is. They have a secret, unperceived and delicate beauty ; he had neede of a cleere, farre-seeing and true-discerning sight that should rightly discover this secret light. . . Socrates maketh his soule to moove, with a naturall and common motion. . .

This man proposeth no vaine fantasies unto himselfe. His end was to store us with things and furnish us with precepts, which really more substantially and joyntly serve our life. . .

So was he ever all one a like : and raised himselfe to the highest pitch of vigor, not by fits, but by complexion. Or to say better, he raised nothing, but rather brought downe and reduced all difficulties or sharpnesse to their originall and naturall state, and thereunto subdued vigor. For in Cato it is manifestly seene to be a forced proceeding, far-above and beyond the common ; by the brave exploits of his life, and in his death, hee is ever perceived to be mounted upon his high horses. Whereas this man keepes on the ground, and with a gentle and ordinary pace treateth of the most profitable discourses, and addresseth himselfe both unto death and to the most thorny and crabbed crosses, that may happen unto the course of humane life. . .

Couragious in his death, not because his soule is immortall, but because he is mortall. A ruinous instruction to all common-weales, and much more harmefull than ingenious and subtile, is that which perswadeth men that onely religious beliefe, and without good conduct, sufficeth to content and satisfie divine justice.

It is a great matter that ever he was able to give such order unto the pure imaginations of a childe, that without altring or wresting them, he hath thence produced the fairest effects of our minde. He neither represents it rich nor high raised, but sound and pure, and ever with a blithe and undefiled health. . .

He it is that brought humane wisedome from heaven againe, where for a long time it had beene lost, to restore it unto man ; where her most just and laborious worke is. . .

He hath done human nature a great kindnesse, to shew what and how much she can doe of her selfe. We are every one richer than we imagine, but we are taught to borrow and instructed to shift ; and rather to make use of others goods and meanes then of our owne.

To what purpose do we so arme and steele our selves with these labouring-efforts of learning ? Let us diligently survay the surface of the earth, and there consider so many poore people as we see toyling, sweltring and drooping about their businesse, which never heard of Aristotle nor of Plato, nor ever knew what exemples or precepts are. From those doth nature dayly draw and afoord us effects of constancy and patternes of patience, more pure and forcible then are those we so curiously study-for in schooles. How many do I ordinarily see that misacknowledge poverty ; how many that wish for death, or that passe it without any alaram or affliction ? A fellow that dungeth my garden hath happily this morning buried his father or his childe.

Civil war

I was writing this about a time that a boistrous storme of our tumultuous broiles and bloody troubles did for many months space, with all it's might and horrour, hang full over my head. . .

O monstrous Warre ! Others worke without, this inwardly and against her selfe, and with her owne venome gnaweth and consumes her selfe. It is of so ruinous and maligne a Nature, that, together with all things else, it ruineth it selfe ; and with spitefull rage doth rent, deface and massacre it selfe. We doe more often see it, by and through it selfe, to wast, to desolate and dissolve it selfe, then by or through want of any necessary thing, or by enemies force. All manner of discipline doth shunne and flie it. She commeth to cure sedition, and her selfe is throughly therewith infected ; she goeth about to chastize disobedience, and sheweth the example of it ; and being employed for the defence of Lawes entreth into actuall rebellion against her owne ordinances. Aye me, where are we ?

Plato likewise is not willing one should offer violence to the quiet repose of his Countrey, no not to reforme or cure the same ; and alloweth not that reformation which disturbeth or hazardeth the whole estate ; and which is purchased with the blood and ruine of the Citizens. . . I was a Platonist on that side before ever I knew there had beene a Plato in the world.

Ambition, avarice, cruelty and revenge have not sufficient proppes and naturall impetuousity ; let us allure and stirre them up by the glorious title of justice and devotion. There can no worse estate of things be imagined than where wickednesse commeth to be lawfull, and with the Magistrates' leave to take the cloake of vertue.

The living were faine to suffer, so did such as then were scarce borne. They were robbed and pilled, and by consequence so was I, even of hope ; spoiling and depriving them of all they had to provide their living for many yeares to come. . .

Besides these mischiefes I endured some others. I incurred the inconveniences that moderation bringeth in such diseases. I was shaven on all hands. To the Ghibelin I was a Guelf, to Guelf a Ghibelin. Some one of my Poets expresseth as much, but I wot not where it is. The situation of my house, and the acquaintance of such as dwelt round about me, presented me with one visage ; my life and actions with another. No formall accusations were made of it, for there was nothing to take hold of. I never opposed my selfe against the lawes, and who had called me in question should have lost by the bargaine. . .

I commonly affoord ayde unto injurious presumption that fortune scattereth against me ; by a fashion I never had, to avoïd justifying, excusing, or interpreting my selfe ; deeming it to be a putting of

my conscience to compromise, to pleade for it:
And as if every man saw into mee as cleare as I doe
my selfe, in lieu of withdrawing, I advance my selfe
to the accusation and rather endeare it by a scoffing
confession, except I flatly hold my peace as of a
thing unworthy any answer. But such as take it
for an over-proud confidence, doe not much lesse
disesteeme and hate me for it, then such as take it
for weaknesse of an indefensible cause. . .

Let us thanke Fortune, that hath not made us live
in an effeminate, idle, and languishing age; As I
reade not much in Histories, these confusions of
other states, without regret, that I could not better
consider them present; so doth my curiosity make
me somewhat please my selfe with mine eyes to see
this notable spectacle of our publike death; its symp-
tomes and formes. And since I could not hinder
the same, I am content to be appointed as an assist-
ant unto it, and therby instruct my selfe. . . I doubt
whether I may lawfully avow at how base a rate of
my lifes rest and tranquility I have past it more than
halfe in the ruine of my Country. In accidents
that touch me not in my freehold I purchase patience
a little too cheape; and to complaine to my selfe I
respect not so much what is taken from mee, as what
is left me both within and without.

Plague

Loe here another huddle or tide of mischiefe, that
on the necke of the former came rushing upon mee.
Both within and round about my house, I was overtaken, in respect of all other, with a most contagious
pestilence. For, as soundest bodies are subject to

grievous diseases, because they onely can force them ; so the aire about me being very healthy, wher n no mans memory infection (although very neere) could ever take footing, comming now to be poisoned, brought forth strange effects. . .

I was faine to endure this strange condition, that the sight of my house was frightful unto me. Whatever was therein lay without guard, and was free to any that had a minde unto it. I who am so hospitable, was much troubled and put to my shifts, how to finde out some retreate for my family — A dismaied and scattered family, making both it selfe and its friends afraide, and breeding horrour where it sought to retire for shelter, having now to shift and change its dwelling, so soone as any of the company beganne to feele his finger ake. Every sicknesse is then taken for the plague : none hath leasure to consider them. And the mischiefe is, that according to rules of arte, what danger soever approcheth, a man must continue forty dayes in anxiety or feare of that evill ; in which time your owne imagination doth perplex you as she list and infect your health. All which had much lesse toucht mee, had I not beene forced to beare other mens burthens and partake all their grievances, and for six months space in miserable maner to be a woefull guide to so great-confused a Caravane. For I ever carry my preservatives about me, which are resolution and sufferance. Apprehension doth not greatly presse me, which is particularly feared in this sicknesse. And if, being alone, I should have taken it, it had beene a much more cheerful and more distant flight. . .

What examples of resolution saw we not then in

all this peoples simplicity ?   Each one generally re
nounced all care of life.   The grapes (which ar
the countries chiefe commoditie) hung still an
rotted upon the vines untouch't ; all indifferently
preparing themselves, and expecting death eithe
that night or the next morrow ; with countenanc
and voice so little daunted, that they seemed to hav
compromitted to this necessitie, and that it was a
universall and inevitable condemnation.   It is eve
such.   But on how little depends resolution in dy
ing ?   The difference and distance of some fe
houres ; the onely consideration of the compan
yeelds the apprehension diverse unto us.   Behol
these ! because they die in one same month, chi
dren, yong, old, they are no more astonied, they ar
no longer wept-for.   I saw some that feared to sta
behinde, as if they had beene in some horrible sol
tude.   And commonly I knew no other care among
them but for graves ; it much grieved them to se
the dead carcasses scattered over the fields, at th
mercy of wilde beasts, which presently began t
flocke thither. . . Some in good health digged a
ready their graves, othersome yet living did go
into them ; and a day-labourer of mine, as he w
dying, with his owne hands and feet pulled eart
upon him, and so covered himselfe.   Was not th
a lying downe in the shade to sleepe at ease ?

Apprehension of Death

If you know not how to die, take no care for it
Nature her selfe will fully and sufficiently teach yo
in the nicke, she will exactly discharge that work

for you ; trouble not your selfe with it. We trouble death with the care of life, and life with the care of death. . . It is not against death we prepare our selves, it is a thing too momentary. A quarter of an houre of passion without consequence and without annoyance deserves not particular precepts. To say truth, we prepare our selves against the preparations of death.

Men are different in feeling and diverse in force ; they must be directed to their good according to themselves, and by diverse waies. . . And is it not as we say, that the vulgars stupidity and want of apprehension affoorde them this patience in private evils, and this deepe carelesnes of sinister future accidents ? That their mind being more grosse, dull and blockish, is lesse penetrable and agitable ? In Gods name, if it be so, let us henceforth keepe a schoole of brutality.

Beauty

Socrates hath beene a perfect patterne in all great qualities, I am vexed that ever he met with so unhansome and crabbed a body as they say he had, and so dissonant from the beauty of his minde. Nature did him wrong. There is nothing more truely likely as the conformity or relation betweene the body and the minde. . . I cannot often enough repeate how much I esteeme beauty, so powerfull and advantagious a quality is it. He named it a short tyranny, And Plato the priviledge of Nature. We have none that exceeds it in credit ; it possesseth the chiefe ranke in the commerce of society of men ; it presents it selfe forward, seduceth and preoccupates our judgement with great authority and wonderfull impression. . . Not onely in men that serve me, but in beasts also, I consider the same within two inches of goodnesse.

Yet me thinkes that the same feature and manner of the face, and those lineaments by which some argue certaine inward complexions and our future fortunes, is a thing that doth not directly nor simply lodge under the chapter of beauty and ill favourdnesse. . . For an ill favourd and ill composed face may sometimes harbour some aire of probity and trust. As on the contrary I have sometimes read between two faire eyes the threats of a maligne and dangerous-ill-boding nature. There are some favourable Physiognomies, For in a throng of victorious enemies you shall presently ammiddest a multitude of unknowne faces, make choise of one man more than of others to yeeld your selfe unto and trust your life, and not properly by the consideration of beauty. . .

I have (as elsewhere I noted) taken for my regard this ancient precept, very rawly and simply : That We cannot erre in following Nature ; and that the soveraigne document is for a man to conforme himselfe to her. I have not (as Socrates), by the power and vertue of reason, corrected my natural complexions, nor by Art hindered mine inclination. As I came into the World, so I goe-on : I strive with nothing. My two Mistress parts live of their owne kindnesse in peace and good agreement ; but my nurses milke hath (thankes be to God) been indifferently wholesome and temperate.

Physiognomy

I have a favourable apparence, both in forme and
in interpretation. It hath often betided me, that by
the simple credit of my presence and aspect, some
that had no knowledge of me have greatly trusted
unto it, were it about their owne affaires or mine.
And even in forraine countries, I have thereby
reaped singular and rare favours.

These two experiences are haply worthy to be
particularly related. A *quidam* gallant determined
upon a time to surprise both my house and my selfe.
His plot was to come riding alone to my gate, and
instantly to urge entrance. I knew him by name,
and had some reason to trust him, being my neigh-
bour and somwhat alide unto me. I presently
caused my gates to be opened, as I do to all men.
He comes-in all afrighted, his horse out of breath ;
both much harassed. He entertaines me with this
fable : that within halfe a league of my house he was
sodainely set-upon by an enemy of his whom I
knew well, and had heard of their quarrell ; that his
foe had wondrously put him to his spurres ; that
being surprised unarmed, and having fewer in his
company than the other, he had made haste to come
to my house, for safety ; That he was much troubled
for his men, all which he supposed to be either taken
or slaine. I endevoured in all simplicity to comfort
and re-assure and refresh him. Within a while came
gallopping foure or five of his Souldiers, amazed,
as if they had beene out of their wits, hasting to be
let-in. Shortly after came others, and others, all
proper men, well mounted, better armed, to the

number of thirty or there abouts, all seeming distracted for feare, as if the enemy that pursued them had beene at their heeles. This mystery beganne to summon my suspicion. I was not ignorant of the age wherein I lived, nor how much my house might be envied; and had sundry examples of others of my acquaintance that had beene spoiled, beset, and surprised thus and thus. So it is, that perceiving with my selfe, there was nothing to be gained by having begunne to use them kindly, if I continued not, and being unable to rid my selfe of them and cleare my house without an open break, I tooke the simplest and most naturall way, as I ever doe, and commanded they should be let-in and bid welcome. And to say truth, I am by nature little suspicious or mistrustfull. I am easily drawen to admit excuses and encline to mild interpretations. I take men according to common order, and do not beleeve these perverse and trecherous inclinations, except I be compelled by some authenticall testimony, no more then monsters or miracles. Besides, I am a man that willingly commit my selfe unto fortune, and carelesly cast my selfe into her armes; whereof hitherto I have more just cause to commend my selfe then to complaine. And have found her more circumspect and friendly-carefull of my affaires then I am my selfe. There are certaine actions in my life, the conduct of which may justly be termed difficult, or if any be so disposed, prudent. And of those, suppose the third part of them to be mine owne, truely the other two are richly hirs.

But to come to my former discourse. These gallants kept still on horsebacke in my court, and would not alight; their Captaine with me in my hall, who

would never have his horse stabled, still saying that
he must necessarily withdraw himselfe so soon as he
had newes of his followers.   He saw himselfe master of his enterprise, and nothing was wanting but
the execution.   Hee hath since reported very often
(for he was no whit scrupulous or afraid to tell this
story) that my lookes, and my frankness of speech
made him reject all manner of treasonable intents
or trecherous desseignes.   What shall I say more ?
He bids me farewell, calleth for his horse, gets up,
and offreth to be gone, his people having continually
their eyes fixed upon him, to observe his lookes and
see what signe he should make unto them ; much
amazed to see him begone, and wondring to see him
omit and forsake such an advantage.

An other time, trusting to a certaine truce or cessation of armes that lately had beene published
through our campes in France, I undertooke a journey from home, through a dangerous and very
ticklish countrey.   I had not rid far but I was discovered, and behold three or foure troupes of horse-
men, all severall wayes, made after me, with purpose to entrap me ; One of which overtooke mee the
third day, where I was round beset and charged by
fifteene or twenty Gentlemen, who had all vizards
and cases, followed by a band of Argoletiers.   I was
charged ; I yeelded ; I was taken and immediately
drawne into the bosome of a thicke Wood that was
not far-off ; there puld from my horse, stripped with
all speed, my truncks and clokebags rifled, my box
taken, my horses, my equipage, and such things as
I had, dispersed and shared amongst them.   We
continued a good while amongst those thorny
bushes, contesting and striving about my ransome,

which they racked so high that it appeared well I was not much knowne of them. They had long contestation among themselves for my life. And to say truth, there were many circumstances threatned me of the danger I was in.

I ever stood upon the title and priviledge of the truce and that I was content to leave them what ever they had taken from me, which was not to be despised, without promising other ransome. After we had debated the matter to and fro the space of two or three houres, and that no excuses could serve, they set me upon a lame jade, which they knew could never escape them, and committed the particular keeping of my person to fifteene or twenty harque-busiers, and dispersed my people to others of their crew, commanding we should all divers wayes be carried prisoners, and my selfe being gone two or threescore paces from them, behold a sodain and unexpected alteration took them. I saw their Captaine comming towards me, with a cheerful countenance and much milder speeches than before, carefully trudging up and down through all the troups to find out my goods againe, which as he found al scattred he forced every man to restore them unto me ; and even my purse and my boxe came to my hands againe. To conclude, the most precious jewell they presented me was my liberty ; as for my other things, I cared not greatly at that time.

What the true cause of so unlookt-for a change and so sodaine an alteration was, without any apparent impulsion, and of so wonderfull repentance, at such a time, in such an opportunity and such an enterprise, fore-meditated, consulted and effected without controlement, and which through custome and the impiety of times was now become lawfull (for at the first brunt I plainely confessed and genuinly told them what side I was of, where my way lay, and whither I was riding), I verily know not yet, nor can I give any reason for it. The chiefest amongst them unmasked himselfe, told me his name, and repeated divers times unto me that I should acknowledge my deliverance to my countenance, to my boldnesse and constancy of speech, and be beholding to them for it, insomuch as they made me unworthy of such a misfortune ; and demanded assurance of me for the like curtesie. It may be that the inscrutable goodnesse of God used this vaine instrument for my preservation ; for the next morrow it also shielded me from worse dangers, whereof themselves gently forewarned me. The last is yet living, able to report the whole successe himselfe ; the other was slaine not long since.

If my countenance had not answered for me, if the ingenuity of mine inward intent might not plainely have been deciphered in mine eyes and voice, surely I could never have continued so long without quarrels or offences : with this indiscreete liberty, to speake freely (be it right or wrong) whatever commeth to my minde, and rashly to judge of things.

Bk. III, ch. 12, *Of Physiognomy*

Laws

Reason hath so many shapes that wee know not which to take hold of. Experience hath as many. The consequence we seeke to draw from the conference of events is unsure, because they are ever

dissemblable. No quality is so universall in this
surface of things as variety and diversity. . . Yet
doth not the opinion of that man greatly please mee,
that supposed by the multitude of lawes to curbe
the authority of judges in cutting out their morsels.
He perceived not that there is as much liberty and
extension in the interpretation of lawes as in their
fashion. . .

We have given our judges so large a scope to
moote, to opinionate, to suppose, and decide, that
there was never so powerfull and so licentious a
liberty. What have our lawmakers gained with
chusing a hundred thousand kinds of particular
cases, and adding as many lawes unto them ? That
number hath no proportion with the infinite diversity of humane actions. The multiplying of our
inventions shall never approach to the variation of
examples. Adde a hundred times as many unto
them, yet shall it not follow that of events to come
there be any one found that in all this infinite number of selected and enregistred events shall meete
with one to which it may so exactly joyne and
match, but some circumstance and diversity will
remaine that may require a diverse consideration of
judgement. There is but little relation betweene
our actions that are in perpetuall mutation and the
fixed and unmoveable lawes. The most to be desired are the rarest, the simplest, and most generall.
And yet I believe it were better to have none at
all then so infinite a number as we have. Nature
gives them ever more happy then those we give our
selves.

Lawyers

Wherefore is it that our common language, so easie to be understood in all other matters, becommeth so obscure, so harsh, and so hard to bee understood in law-cases, bils, contracts, indentures, citations, wils, and testaments? And that hee who so plainely expresseth himselfe, what ever he speaks or writes of any other subject, in law matters findes no manner or way to declare himselfe or his meaning that admits not some doubt or contradiction; unlesse it be that the Princes of this art, applying themselves with a particular attention to invent and chuse strange, choise, and solemne words, and frame artificiall cunning clauses, have so plodded and poized every syllable, canvased and sifted so exquisitely every seame and quiddity, that they are now so entangled and so confounded in the infinity of figures and so severall-small partitions, that they can no more come within the compasse of any order, or prescription, or certaine understanding.

Commentaries

It was never seene that two men judged alike of one same thing: And it is impossible to see two opinions exactly semblable, not onely in divers men, but in any one same man at severall houres. I commonly find something to doubt-of, where the commentary happily never deigned to touch, as deeming it so plaine. I stumble sometimes as much in an even smooth path, as some horses that I know who oftner trip in a faire plaine way than in a rough and

stony. Who would not say that glosses increase
doubts and ignorance, since no booke is to be seene,
whether divine or profane, commonly read of all
men, whose interpretation increaseth not the difficulty? The hundredth commentary sends it to
its succeeder more thorny and more crabbed than
the first found it. When agreed we amongst our
selves to say, this booke has enough; there's now
nothing more to be said of it?

There's more adoe to enterpret interpretations
than to interpret things, and more bookes upon
bookes then upon any other subject. We do but
enter-glose our selves. All swarmeth with com-
mentaries; of Authors there is great penury.

Liberty

No judge hath yet, God be thanked, spoken to
me as a judge in any cause whatsoever, either mine
or another mans, criminal or civill. No prison did
ever receive me, no not so much as for recreation to
walke in. The very imagination of one maketh the
sight of their outside seeme irkesome and loathsome
to mee. I am so besotted unto liberty that should
any man forbid me the accesse unto any one corner
of the Indiaes I should in some sort live much dis-
contented. And so long as I shall finde land or open
aire elsewhere, I shall never lurke in any place where
I must hide my selfe. Oh God, how hardly could
I endure the miserable condition of so many men,
confined and immured in some corners of this king-
dome, barred from entring the chiefest Cities, from
accesse into Courts, from conversing with men, and

interdicted the use of common wayes, onely because they have offended our lawes. If those under which I live should but threaten my fingers end, I would presently goe finde out some others, wheresoever it were. All my small wisedome, in these civill and tumultuous warres wherein we now live, doth wholly employ it selfe, that they may not interrupt my liberty to goe and come where ever I list. Lawes are now maintained in credit, not because they are essentially just, but because they are lawes. It is the mysticall foundation of their authority — they have none other. . . There is nothing so grossely and largely offending, nor so ordinarily wronging as the Lawes. Whosoever obeyeth them because they are just, obeyes them not justly the way as he ought.

Nature's rules

With great reason doe philosophers addresse us unto natures rules ; but they have nought to doe with so sublime a knowledge ; They falsifie them, and present her to us with a painted face, too-high in colour and overmuch sophisticated ; whence arise so many different pourtraits of so uniforme a subject. As she hath given us feete to goe withall, so hath she endowed us with wisedome to direct our life.

For a man to commit himselfe most simply unto nature is to doe it most wisely. Oh how soft, how gentle, and how sound a pillow is ignorance and incuriosity to rest a well composed head upon.

Judgement

Judgement holds in me a presidentiall seate, at least it carefully endevours to hold it ; it suffers my appetits to keep their course, both hatred and love, yea and that I beare unto my selfe, without suffering alteration or corruption. If it can not reforme other parts according to itselfe, at least it will not be deformed by them ; it keepes its court apart. . . For some degree of intelligence is required to be able to marke that one is ignorant, and wee must knocke at a gate to know whether it bee shutte. . . Affirmation and selfe-conceit are manifest signes of foolishnesse.

Inconsequence

I doe not onely find it difficult to combine our actions one unto another ; but take every one apart, it is hard by any principall quality to desseigne the same properly, so double, so ambiguous and party-coloured, are they to divers lusters. . .

No maner of going without crosse and strange contrarieties ; no faculty simple ; so that the likeliest a man may one day conclude of him, shall be that he affected and laboured to make himselfe knowne by being not to bee knowne. . .

Way of life and personal habits

A yong man should disturb his rules to stirre-up his vigor, and take heed he suffer not the same to grow faint or sluggish ; for there is no course of life so weake and foolish as that which is mannaged by Order, Methode, and Discipline.

If he beleeve me he shall often even give himselfe unto excesse ; otherwise the least disorder wil utterly overthrow him, and so make him unfit and unwelcome in conversation. . .

Although I have (as much as might bee) beene inured to liberty and fashioned to indifferency, yet in growing aged I have through carelesnesse relied more upon certaine formes (my age is now exempted from institution, and hath not any thing else to looke unto but to maintaine it selfe) which custome hath already, without thinking on it, in certaine things so wel imprinted her character in me, that I deeme it a kind of excesse to leave them. And without long practise I can neither sleepe by day, nor eate betweene meales, nor break my fast, nor goe to bed without some entermission (as of three houres after supper) . . . nor beare mine owne sweate, nor quench my thirst either with cleere water or wine alone, nor continue long bareheaded, nor have mine hair cut after dinner. And I could as hardly spare my gloves as my shirt, or forbeare washing of my hands both in the morning and rising from the table ; or lye in a bed without a testerne and curtaines about it, as of most necessary things. I could dine without a table-cloth, but hardly without a cleane napkin, as Germans commonly doe. I foule and sully them more then either they or the Italians, and I seldome use eyther spoone or forke. I am sory we follow not a custome which, according to the example of Kings, I have seene begunne by some, that upon every course or change of dish, as we have shift of cleane trenchers, so we might have change of cleane napkins. We read that that laborious souldier Marius, growing olde, grew more nicely delicate in his drinking, and would taste no drincke except in a peculiar cuppe of his. As for me, I observe a kinde of like methode in glasses, and of one certaine forme, and drinke not willingly in a common-glasse, no more than of one ordinary hand. I mislike all manner of metall in regard of a bright transparent matter : let mine eyes also have taste of what I drinke according to their capacity. I am beholding to custome for many such nicenesses and singularities. Nature hath also on the other side bestowed this upon me, that I can not wel brooke two full meales in one day without surcharging my stomacker ; nor the meere abstinence of one without filling my selfe with winde, drying my mouth, and dulling my appetite. . .

Sickness and health

Both in health and in sicknesse I have willingly seconded and given my selfe over to those appetites that pressed me. I allow great authority to my desires and propensions. I love not to cure one evill by another mischiefe. I hate those remedies that importune more than sicknesse. To be subject to the cholike, and to be tied to abstaine from the pleasure I have in eating of oysters, are two mischiefes for one. The disease pincheth us the one side, the rule on the other. Since we are ever in danger to misdoe, let us rather hazard our selves to follow pleasure. Most men doe contrary and thinke nothing profitable that is not painefull ; facility is by them suspected. Mine appetite hath in divers things very happily accommodated and ranged it selfe to the health of my stomake. Being yong, acrimony and tartnesse in sawces did greatly delight me, but my stomacke being since glutted therewith, my taste hath likewise seconded the same. Wine hurts the sicke ; it is the first thing that with an invincible distaste brings my mouth out of taste. Whatsoever I receive unwillingly or distastefully, hurts me, whereas nothing doth it whereon I feed with hunger and rellish. I never received harme by any action that was very pleasing unto me. And yet I have made all medicinall conclusions largely to yeeld to my pleasures.

We must gently obey and endure the lawes of our condition. We are subject to grow aged, to become weake and to fall sicke, in spight of all physicke.

A man must learne to endure that patiently which he cannot avoyde conveniently. Our life is composed, as is the harmony of the World, of contrary things ; so of divers tunes, some pleasant, some harsh, some sharpe, some flat, some low, and some high. What would that Musition say that should love but some one of them ? He ought to know how to use them severally and how to entermingle them. So should we both of goods and evils which are consubstantiall to our life. Our being cannot subsist without this commixture, whereto one side is no lesse necessary than the other.

Convalescence

But is there anything so pleasant in respect of this sodaine change when by an extreame paine I come by the voyding of my stone, to recover, as from a lightning, the faire Sunne-shine of health ; so free and full, as it happeneth in our sodaine and most violent cholliks ? Is there anything in this paine suffered that may be counter poised to the sweet pleasure of so ready an amendment ? By how much more health seemeth fairer unto me after sicknesse, so neere and so contiguous, that I may know them in presence one of another, in their richest ornaments. . .

There is so much hazard and so many degrees before one can be brought to safety, that hee is never at an end. Before you can leave off your cover-chiefe and then your nightcap, before you can brooke the ayre againe or have leave to drinke Wine, or lye with your Wife, or eate melons, it is much if you fall not into some relapse or new misery.

Personal habits

Nothing ought so much be recommended unto youth as activity and vigilancy. Our life is nothing but motion, I am hardly shaken, and am slow in all things, be it to rise, to goe to bed, or to my meales. Seaven of the clocke in the morning is to me an early houre ; and where I may command, I neither dine before eleven, nor sup till after six. I have heretofore imputed the cause of agues or maladies, whereinto I have falne, to the lumpish heavinesse or drowzy dulnesse which my long sleeping had caused me. And ever repented mee to fall asleepe againe in the morning. Plato condemnes more the excesse of sleeping then the surfet of drinking. I love to lie hard and alone, yea and without a woman by me, after the kingly manner ; somewhat well and warme covered. I never had my bed warmed, but since I came to be an old man, if need require, I have clothes given me to warme my feete and my stomacke.

If there bee any curiosity in my behaviour or manner of life, it is rather about my going to bed then any thing else ; but if neede bee, I generally yeeld and accommodate my selfe unto necessity, as well and as quietly, as any other whosoever. Sleeping hath possessed a great part of my life ; and as old as I am, I can sleepe eight or nine houres together. I doe with profit withdraw my selfe from this sluggish propension, and evidently finde my selfe better by it. Indeede, I somewhat feele the stroke of alteration, but in three dayes it is past. And I see few that live with lesse (when need is), and that more constantly exercise themselves, nor whom toyling and labour offend lesse. My body is capable of a firme agitation, so it be not vehement and sodaine. I avoide violent exercises, and which induce mee to sweate ; my limbs will sooner be wearied then heated. I can stand a whole day long, and am seldome weary with walking. Since my first age, I ever loved rather to ride then walke upon paved streets. Going a foote, I shall durty my selfe up to my waste ; and little men, going alongst our streets, are subject (for want of presentiall apparence) to be justled or elbowed.

The military life

No profession or occupation is more pleasing then the military : a profession or exercise both noble in execution (for the strongest, most generous

and prowdest of all vertues, is true valour) and noble
in it's cause. No utility, either more just or universall then the protection of the repose or defence
of the greatnesse of ones country. The company
and dayly conversation of so many noble, young,
and active men, cannot but bee well-pleasing to you ;
the dayly and ordinary sight of so divers tragicall
spectacles ; the liberty and uncontroled freedome
of that artelesse and unaffected conversation, mascu-
line and ceremonilesse maner of life ; the hourely
variety of a thousand ever changing and differing
actions ; the couragious and minde stirring harmony
of warlike musicke, which at once entertaineth with
delight and enflameth with longing, both your eares
and your minde ; the imminent and matchlesse honour of that exercise ; yea the very sharpnesse and
difficulty of it. . .

Natural content

Were my body directed by me, as is my minde,
we should march a little more at our ease. I
had it then, not onely exempted from all trouble,
but also full of satisfaction and blithenesse, as it is
most commonly, partly by it's owne complexion,
and partly by it's owne desseigne . . . nor doe I
complaine of the naturall decadence that possesseth
me.

No more then I grieve that my continuance is not
as long and sound as that of an oake. I have no
cause to finde fault with my imagination. I have
in my life had very few thoughts or cares that have
so much as interrupted the course of my sleepe, except desire which awakened without afflicting me.

I seldome dreame, and when I doe, it is of extravagant things and chymeras, commonly produced of pleasant conceits, rather ridiculous then sorrowfull. And thinke it true that dreames are the true interpreters of our inclinations ; but great skill is required to sort and understand them.

Personal tastes

I stand not much on nice choice of meates at the table, and commonly begin with the first and neerest dish, and leape not willingly from one taste to another. Multitude of dishes and variety of services displease me as much as any other throng. I am easily pleased with few messes, and hate the opinion of Favorinus, that at a banquet you must have that dish whereon you feed hungerly taken from you, and ever have a new one set in the place : And that it is a niggardly supper if all the guests be not glutted with pinions and rumps of divers kinds of fowle, and that onely the dainty bird beccafico or snapfig deserveth to bee eaten whole at one morsell. I feede much upon salt cates, and love to have my bread somewhat fresh. And mine owne Baker makes none other for my bord, against the fashion of my country. In my youth my overseers had much a doe to reforme the refusall I made of such meats as youth doth commonly love best ; as sweet meates, confets and marchpanes. My Tutor was wont to find great fault with my lothing of such dainties, as a kinde of squeamish delicacy. And to say truth, it is nothing but a difficulty of taste, where it once is applyed. Whosoever remooveth from a child a certaine particular or obstinate affection to browne bread, to bakon, or to garlike, taketh friandize from him. There are some that make it a labour and thinke it a patience to regret a good piece of pawdred beefe, or a good gemmon of bakon, amongst partridges. Are not they wise men in the meane time? It is the chiefe dainty of all dainties; It is the taste of nice effeminate fortune that wil be distasted with ordinary and usual things.

Indeede there is this difference, that it is better for one to tye his desires unto things easiest to be gotten, yet is it a vice to tie himselfe to any strict-nesse.

Long sitting at meales doth much weary and dis-temper me, for be it for want of better countenance and entertainment, or that I used my selfe unto it when I was a child, I feede as long as I sitte at the table. And therefore, being in mine owne house, though my board be but short and that wee use not to sit long, I doe not commonly sit downe with the first, but a pretty while after others. Con-trary, I love to sit a great while after, and to heare some discourse or table-talke. Alwayes provided I beare not a part my selfe, for if my belly bee full I shall soone be weary and hurt my selfe with talk-ing, and I finde the exercise of lowde-speaking and contesting before meate very pleasant and whole-some. . . Such as have care of me may easily steale from me what soever they imagine may be hurtfull for me, inasmuch as about my feeding I never desire or find fault with that I see not. But if a dish or any thing else be once set before me, they lose their labour that goe about to tell me of abstinence; so that when I am disposed to fast I must be sequestred from eaters, and have no more set before me than may serve for a stinted and regular collation ; for if I but sit downe at a set table I forget my resolution. If I chance to bidde my cooke change the dressing of some kinde of meate or dish, all my men know my appetit is sickly, and I shall hardly touch it. I love all manner of flesh or fowle but greene rosted and raw sodden, namely, such as may beare it without danger, and love to have them thoroughly mortified, and in divers of them the very alteration of their smell. Onely hardnesse or toughnesse of meate doth generally molest me, (of all other qualities I am as carelesse and can as well brooke them as any man that ever I knew,) so that (contrary to received opinion) even amongst fishes I shall finde some both too new and over-hard and firme. It is not the fault or want of teeth, which I ever had as perfectly-sound and compleate as any other man, and which but now, being olde, beginne to threaten me. I have from my infancy learn'd to rubbe them with my napkin, both in the morning when I rise and sitting down and rising from the table.

God doth them a grace from whom by little and little he doth substract their life. It is the onely benefit of old age. Their last death shall be so much the lesse full, languishing and painefull, it shall then kill but one halfe or a quarter of a man. Even now I lost one of my teeth, which of it selfe fell out without strugling or paine : it was the naturall terme of it's continuance. That part of my being with divers others, are already dead and mortified in mee, others of the most active, halfe dead, and which during the vigor of my age held the first ranke. Thus I sinke and scape from my selfe . . . verely I receive a speciall comfort in thinking on my death, and that it shall be of the most just and naturall, and cannot now require or hope other favor of destiny concerning that then unlawfull. Men perswade themselves that, as heretofore, they have had a higher stature, so their lives were longer; but they are deceived, for Solon, of those ancient times, though he were of an exceeding high stature, his life continued but seventy yeeres.

Early education

Had I any male-children I should willingly wish them my fortune. That good Father it pleased God to allot me (who hath nothing of mee but thankefulnesse for his goodnesse, which indeed is as great as great may be) even from my cradle sent mee to be brought-up in a poore village of his, where he kept me so long as I suckt, and somewhat longer, breeding me after the meanest and simplest-common fashion.

Never take unto your selfe, and much lesse never give your wives the charge of your childrens breeding or education. Let fortune frame them under the popular and naturall Lawes; Let custome enure them to frugality and breed them to hardnesse: That they may rather descend from sharpenesse than ascend unto it. His conceipt aymed also at another end, To acquaint and re-aly me with that people and condition of men that have most need of us; And thought I was rather bound to respect those which extend their armes unto me than such as turne their backe toward me. And that was the reason he chose no other gossips to hold me at the font than men of abject and base fortune, that so I might

the more be bound and tied unto them. His purpose hath not altogether succeded ill. I willingly
give and accost my selfe unto the meaner sort,
whether it be because there is more glory gotten
by them, or through some naturall compassion,
which in me is infinitely powerfull.

Long life

Shal I, that have so much and so universally adored
that ἄριστον μέτρον, a meane is best, of former times,
and have ever taken a meane measure for the most
perfect, therefore pretend a most prodigious and
unmeasureable life? whatsoever commeth contrary
to Natures course may be combersome, but what
comes according to her should ever please.

Death entermedleth and every where confounds
it self with our life; declination doth preoccupate
her houre and insinuate it selfe in the very course
of our advancement. I have pictures of mine owne
that were drawne when I was five and twenty, and
others being thirty yeeres of age, which I often compare with such as were made by me as I am now at
this instant. How many times doe I say I am no
more my selfe; how much is my present image
further from those then from that of my decease?
It is an over-great abuse unto nature to dragge and
hurry her so farre that she must be forced to give
us over, and abandon our conduct, our eyes, our
teeth, our legges and the rest, to the mercy of a forraine help and begged assistance; and to put our
selves into the hands of art, weary to follow us.

I am not over-much or greedily desirous of sallets
or of fruits, except melons. My father hated all

manner of sawces; I love them all. Over-much eating doth hurt and distemper me, but for the quality I have yet no certaine knowledge that any meate offends me; I never observe either a full or waned Moone, nor make a difference betweene the Spring time or Autumne. There are certaine inconstant and unknowne motions in us. For (by way of example) I have heretofore found radishrootes to be very good for mee, then very hurtfull, and now againe very well agreeing with my stomacke. In divers other things I feele my appetit to change, and my stomacke to diversifie from time to time. I have altred my course of drinking, sometimes from white to claret wine, and then from claret to white againe.

I am very friand and gluttonous of fish, and keepe my shroving dayes upon fish dayes, and my feasts upon fasting-dayes. I believe as some others doe, that fish is of lighter digestion than flesh. As I make it a conscience to eate flesh upon a fish day, so doth my taste to eate fish and flesh together. The diversity betweene them seemes to mee over-distant.

Even from my youth I was wont now and then to miss some repast, either that I might sharpen my stomake against the next day; (for as Epicurus was wont to fast, and made but sparing meales, thereby to accustome his voluptuousnesse to neglect plenty; I, contrary to him, to enure my sensuality to speede the better, and more merrily to make use of plenty) or else I fasted, the better to maintaine my vigor for the service or performance of some bodily or mentall action; for both are strangely dulled in me, through over-much fulnesse and repleatenesse. (And above all, I hate that foolish combination of so sound and bucksome a Goddesse with that indigested and belching God, all puffed with the fume of his liquor) ; or to recover my sick stomake ; or because I lacked some good company. And I say as Epicurus said, that A man should not so much respect what he eateth as with whom he eateth. And commend Chilon, that he would not promise to come to Perianders feast before he knew certainely who were the other bidden guests. No viands are so sweetly pleasing, no sauce so tastefull, as that which is drawne from conversable and mutuall society.

Right enjoyment of sensualities

My selfe, who but grovell on the ground, hate that kinde of human Wisedome which would make us disdainefull and enemies of the bodies culture and pleasure. I deeme it an equall injustice either to take naturall sensualities against the hart, or to take them too neere the hart. . .

There are some (as Aristotle saith) who, with a savage kinde of stupidity, will seeme distastefull, or squemish of them. Some others I know that doe it out of ambition. Why renounce they not also breathing ? why live they not of their own, and refuse light, because it commeth of gratuity and costs them neither invention nor vigor ? That Mars, or Pallas, or Mercurie should nourish them to see, instead of Ceres, Venus, or Bacchus ?

I hate that we should be commanded to have our minds in the clouds whilst our bodies are sitting at the table ; yet would I not have the minde to be fastned thereunto, nor stagnate in it, but I would have it apply it selfe thereunto.

When I dance, I dance ; and when I sleepe, I sleepe. And when I am solitarie walking in a faire orchard, if my thoughts have a while entertained themselve with strange occurrences, I doe another while bring them to walke with mee in the orchard, and to be partakers of the pleasure of that solitari-nesse and of my selfe. Nature hath like a kinde mother observed this, that such actions as shee for our necessities hath enjoyned unto us should also be voluptuous unto us, and doth not onely by reason but also by appetite envite us unto them ; it were injustice to corrupt her rules.

What egregious fooles are we ? Hee hath past his life in idlenesse, say we ; alas ! I have done noth-ing this day. What ? have you not lived ? It is not onely the fundamentall, but the noblest of your occupation. Had I beene placed or thought fit for the managing of great affaires, I would have shewed what I could have performed. Have you knowen how to meditate and mannage your life ? you have accomplished the greatest worke of all. For a man to shew and exploit himselfe nature hath no neede of fortune ; she equally shewes herselfe upon all grounds, in all sutes, before and behinde, as it were without curteines, welt, or gard. Have you knowne how to compose your conduct ? you have done more than he who hath composed bookes. Have you knowne how to take rest ? you have done more than he who hath taken Empires and Citties. The glori-ous masterpiece of man is to live properly.

To live well

So have wise men lived. And that inimitable contention unto vertue which so amazeth us in both Catoes, their so strictly-severe humor, even unto importunity, hath thus mildly submitted it selfe, and taken pleasure in the lawes of human condition and in Venus and Bacchus.

Easie-yeelding and facility doth, in my conceit, greatly honour and is best befitting a magnanimos and noble minde. Epaminondas thought it no scorne to thrust himselfe amongst the boyes of his citie and dance with them, yea, and to sing and play, and with attention busie himselfe, were it in things that might derogate from the honor and reputation of his glorious victories, and from the perfect reformation of manners that was in him. And amongst so infinite admirable actions of Scipio the grand father, a man worthy to be esteemed of heavenly race, nothing addeth so much grace unto him as to see him carelesly to dallie and childishly to trifle in gathering and chusing of cockle-shels, and play at cost castle along the seashoare with his friend Laelius ; and if it were fowle weather, amusing and solacing himselfe to represent in writing and comedies the most popular and base actions of men.

There is nothing so goodly, so faire, and so lawfull, as to play the man well and duely ; Nor Science so hard and difficult as to know how to live this life well. And of all the infirmities we have the most savage is to despise our being.

I enjoyne my mind, with a looke equally regular, to behold both sorrow and voluptuousnesse : and equally constant : but the one merrily and the other severely ; and to be as carefull to extinguish the one, as diligent to extend the other.

Value of life

This vulgar phrase of passe time and to passe the time, represents the custome of those wise men who thinke to have no better account of their life then to passe it over and escape it ; to passe it over and bawke it, and so much as in them lyeth to ignore and avoyd it, as a thing of an yrkesome, tedious, and to bee disdained quality. But I know it to bee otherwise, and finde it to be both priseable and commodious, yea in her last declination, where I hold it. And Nature hath put the same into our hands, furnished with such and so favourable circumstances that if it presse and molest us, or if unprofitably it escape us, we must blame our selves. And yet I prepare and compose my selfe to forgoe and lose it without grudging ; but as a thing that is loseable and transitory by its owne condition, not as troublesome and importunate.

There is a kinde of husbandry in knowing how to enjoy it. I enjoy it double to others. For the measure in enjoyment dependeth more or lesse on the application we lend it. Especially at this instant, that I perceive mine to be short in time, I wil extend it in weight ; I wil stay the promptitude of its flight by the promptitude of my grasp, and by the vigor in using it compensate the haste of its fleeting. According as the possession of life is more short, I must endeavour to make it more profound and full. Other men feele the sweetnesse of contentment and prosperity. I feele it as well as they, but it is not in passing and gliding ; it should be studied, tasted and ruminated so as thereby to yeeld condigne thanks, to him who grants it unto us. They enjoy other pleasures, as that of sleepe, without knowing them. To the end that even sleepe should not thus dully and unfeelingly escape me, and that I might better taste and be acquainted with it, I have in other days found it good to bee troubled and interrupted in the same. I consult with myself over a content-ment, which contentment, I doe not superficially skim, but sound the same, and apply my reason to entertaine and receive it. . . Doe I finde my selfe in some quiet moode ? is there any sensuality that tickles me ? I doe not suffer the same to dally about my sences, but associate my mind unto it. Not to engage or plunge it selfe therein, but therein to take delight ; not to lose, but therein to finde it selfe. And for her part I employ her to view her-selfe in that prosperous state, to ponder and esteeme the good fortune she hath, and to amplifie the same. She measureth how much she is beholding unto God, for that she is at rest with her conscience and other intestine passions, and hath her body in its natural health ; orderly and fully enjoying the flattering and gentle functions, with which it pleaseth him of his grace to recompence the griefes wherewith his justice at his pleasure smiteth us. Oh, how availfull is it unto her to be so seated, that wherever she casteth her eyes, the heavens are calme round about her, and no desire, no feare, or doubt, troubleth the ayre before her ; here is no difficulty over which her imagination passeth not and without offence.

As for me, then, I love my life and cherish it, such

as it hath pleased God to graunt it us. I desire not to complain of the necessity of eating and drinking. Nor that we should sustaine our selves by only putting a little of that drugge into our mouth wherewith Epimenedes was wont to alay hunger, and yet maintained himselfe. Nor that wee should insensibly produce children at our fingers endes or at our heeles. . . Nor that the body should be voyde of desire and without tickling delight. They are ungratefull and impious complaints. I cheerefully and thankefully, and with a good heart, accept what nature hath created for me, and am there with well pleased and am proud of it. Great wrong is offered unto that great and all-puissant Giver, to refuse his gift, which is so absolutely good ; and disanull or disfigure the same. . .

Nature is a gentle guide, yet not more gentle then prudent and just. I quest after her track ; we have confounded her with artificiall traces.

Is it not an errour to esteeme some actions lesse worthy forsomuch as they are necessary ? Yet shall they never remove out of my head that it is not a most convenient marriage to wedde Pleasure unto Necessity. With which (saith an antient Writer) the Gods doe ever complot and consent.

To what end doe wee by a divorce dismember a frame contexted with so mutuall, coherent and brotherly correspondency. Contrariwise, let us repaire and renue the same by enterchangeable offices, that the spirit may awake and quicken the dul heavinesse of the body, and the body stay the lightnesse of the spirit, and settle and fixe the same.

There is no part or parcell unworthy of our care in that present which God hath bestowed upon us.

We are accoumptable even for the least haire of it.
And is it not farcical for any man to direct man according to his condition ; it is simple, naturall, and
the Creator hath seriously and severely given the
same unto us.

I here touch not nor doe I blend with that rabble
or raskality of men, as wee are, nor with that vanity
of desires and cogitations which divert us, those
venerable mindes elevated by fervency of devotion
and earnestnesse of religion, to a constant and con-
sciencious meditation of heavenly-divine things. . .
and who disdaine to rely on our necessitous, fleeting,
and ambiguous commodities ; and easily resigne the
care and use of sensuall and temporall feeding unto
the body.

They will be exempted from them and escape
man. It is meere folly ; insteade of transforming
themselves into Angels, they trans-change themselves into beastes ; in lieu of advancing, they abase
themselves. Such transcending humours affright
me as much as steepy, high, and inaccessible places.
And I finde nothing so hard to be disgested in Socrates his life as his extasies and communication with
Demons. Nothing so human in Plato as that for
which they say hee is called divine. And of our
sciences those which are raised and extolled for the
highest seeme to me the most basest and terrestriall.
I finde nothing so humble and mortall in Alexanders
life as his fancies about his deification. Philotas by
his answer quipped at him very pleasantly and wittily. Hee had by a letter rejoyced that the Oracle
of Jupiter Hammon had placed him amongst the
Gods ; to whom he answered, that in respect and
consideration of him he was very glad ; but yet there

was some cause those men should be pittyed that were to live with a man and obay him who outwent others, and would not bee contented with the state and condition of mortall man.

It is an absolute perfection, and as it were divine for a man to know how to enjoy his being loyally. We seeke for other conditions because we understand not the use of ours, and goe out of our selves forsomuch as we know not what abiding there is. It is vain to get upon stilts, for be wee upon them, yet must we goe with our owne legges.   And sit we upon the highest throne of the World, yet sit we upon our owne taile.   The best and most commendable lives and best pleasing men are (in my conceit) those which are fitted to the common mould and human model, without wonder or extravagancy.   Now hath old age need to be handled more tenderly.   Let us recommend it unto that God who is the protector of health and fountaine of all wisedome, but blithe and social :

Bk. III, ch. 13, *Of Experience*

THE END OF THE THIRD AND LAST BOOKE

BENJAMIN FRANKLIN

CHESTERTON

ANATOLE

WALPOLE

OSCAR WILDE

GOLDSMITH

BACON

SHAKE

Michel Eyquem, Seigneur de Montaigne, was born February 28, 1533, the son of a fish merchant. After a careful education at home, he studied law at Toulouse and was a counsellor in the Court of Assistance of Périgueux, later merged with the Parlement of Bordeaux. He traveled a year in Germany and Italy and was mayor of Bordeaux from 1581 to 1585. Montaigne was one of the first supporters of Henri IV. He died on September 13, 1592.